AN OLD COUNTRY GIRL'S DREAMS GO ON

My First 90 Years – Book 3

Bonnie Lacey Krenning

2022 © Starla Enterprises, Inc.

For information regarding permission, write to:
Starla Enterprises, Inc.
Attention: Permissions Department,
740 W. 2nd, Ste. 200, Wichita, KS 67203

First Edition

ISBN: 9798411713909

Edited by Starla Criser

Printed in the U.S.A.

DEDICATION

This story collection of my memories is a result of my life with many precious people.

My husband, William "Bill" John Krenning, supported and loved me for fifty-eight years. Not a day goes by that I don't think of him and our life together.

My children— John, Charlie, Kathie, and Suzie—helped give my life meaning. They have always made me proud to be their mother.

My grandchildren, great-grandchildren, and great-great-grandchildren are a special blessing that I will always treasure.

My parents, Anna and Herbert Lacey, made me into the woman I am today. They lived through difficult times but never gave up. They loved each of their many children. And they showed us not only to survive but to thrive, to appreciate, and to have fun and laugh.

ABOUT BONNIE LACEY KRENNING

After nearly nine decades of living, Bonnie is still going strong. She has led a challenging life and continues to treasure each day given to her.

Her husband, Bill, was her soulmate for fifty-eight years before he passed. Their family of four grown children, seven grandchildren, ten great-grandchildren, and two great-great-grandchildren are of key importance in her life.

Throughout her life, she has had many helpful pleasures, including sewing, gardening, and redecorating. Her dream of being a nurse since age six became a reality at age forty-eight.

Upon that graduation, Bill bought her a Cessna 150 as a special gift. Not long after that, at age fifty, she had the chance to fulfill another of her dreams, that of being a pilot.

In their many years toether, Bonnie and Bill had the opportunities to vacation throughout the united States. and she had the chance to go on mision trips to Ephesus and China.

TABLE OF CONTENTS

Chapter One
THE DREAM BEGINS

Childhood Dreams.

_X_Marry a good-looking man and have good-looking children.

_X_Have two boys and two girls.

___Be a nurse.

___Fly an airplane.

From the time I was five years old, I already knew what I wanted. I wanted my own house and my own husband. I wanted just four children, two boys and two girls, since I had so many brothers (ten) and a sister,

I believed I was plain looking with short, straight, brown hair and suntanned skin. Some little girls I knew had blonde, curly hair, blue eyes, and pink skin. My husband would be good looking so I could have good-looking kids. And my husband must own a candy store, so I could have all the candy I wanted and not have to share it with all my siblings.

Also, I would be a nurse. An older brother was a medic in the Army. He showed me a book that showed me what we look like inside. I couldn't read it, but I liked the pictures. I asked him what girls do where he works. He said they called them "nurses." They took care of sick people. I wanted to do that when I grew up.

1949 Bonnie and Bill

Dreams on Hold.

Because of the lack of resources and meeting Bill at sixteen and falling in love with him, my dreams got delayed. But not forgotten. We got married when I was eighteen. That deviated from my childhood dream. I had planned not to get married until I was twenty-five years old.

Most importantly, our family always came first with me: Bill and our four kids. John (Johnnie) Herbert, Charles William (Charlie), Kathryn (Kathi) Ann, and Susan (Suzie)

Carol have always been the biggest treasures in my life. And church was a priority, too.

As our kids grew, I was involved in their school activities and watching after them. I loved being a homemaker and all the joys and responsibilities which came with it. My mother had been a special woman and gave tirelessly all her life to taking care of her family. I wanted to be like her.

I also liked sewing and the "businesswoman" side it brought to me over the first years of our marriage. With all of this, there just wasn't time for nursing school in those early years.

Bill liked that I put our family first, but he knew I wanted to become a nurse someday. I often talked with him about my dream. Usually, it seemed like he wasn't listening. He wasn't a man who said a lot.

Bedpans?

One day, Bill surprised me and said, "You've worked hard all your life. Why don't you just take it easy now?" Then he added, "But if that's what it takes to make you happy, okay. I don't know why you would want to be a nurse and empty bedpans!" He scrunched his nose as he made the comment.

I understood he wasn't being mean. He just worried about me. He later learned first-hand the truth about nursing and all that a nurse does.

Regulations and Decisions.

In 1965, as I approached thirty-five years of age, I heard about a federal regulation that would affect my plans. It restricted a person, mostly women, from starting college after age thirty-five for a Bachelor of Science in Nursing degree (BSN).

Our kids were now young teenagers. Not wanting to lose out on trying to reach for my dream, I decided to begin at Wichita State University (WSU) for my degree.

It had been close to twenty years since I graduated from high school. The school was small, and I didn't major in the sciences and math, the basics of nursing. So, I was concerned. When I took the entrance exam, though, I scored in the nineties, a great relief.

Because I had such a busy life with my family, I only took two, three-hour classes the first semester. I got an "A" in both and was proud of my accomplishment. I could do this! I had come a long way from having trouble learning to read as a child. Daddy had been so patient with me, when my teachers were frustrated. It wasn't until years later that I realized I was dyslexic. But that problem has never stopped me.

At about the same time, I heard the regulation for starting nursing school after age thirty-five was lifted. By now, our kids had learned to do their fair share of work around the house. And they were pleased and excited that their mom was going to college. Bill not so much, but he quietly went along with it.

Stepping Back for Now.

After a full semester in college, I felt I missed out on too much of our kids' school and church activities. Since the age regulation wasn't a problem now, I put that dream on hold, deciding I would wait until the kids were grown up and independent before going back to finish my nursing degree.

Also, there was the financial side of it to consider. Bill and I had never discussed the cost of college and paying for it. The fee was $12 per credit hour. I wanted to pay as I went, and I started saving to cover the cost. I didn't plan for Bill to pay for my nursing school dream. He did enough for our family.

Earlier in our marriage, I thought we needed two joint checking accounts: one for Bill, one for me. My reasoning was that when Bill wrote checks, the balance had to be accurate to the penny. When I wrote checks, if the balance was off a few cents or a couple of dollars, it was okay with me. That annoyed him. He would figure out my mistakes and make the needed corrections.

Our plan worked well for us. We each wrote checks on our particular checking account. I sometimes needed to write checks on his account, making sure the figures were accurate to the penny. My checks were a floral design; his were a plain pattern. He didn't want to use mine, too girly.

Determined not to put a strain on our family's finances, I started saving for college. Susan had started working at a fast-food store while in high school, and she soon became the manager. We were very proud of her. Then she helped me out by hiring me for part-time work so I could reach my goal of paying for college.

Babysitting Time.

Keeping my goal in the back of my mind, I still always made time for our family, especially our grandkids. Kathi and her husband Bob lived across the street from us when their firstborn, Jeremy, was a baby. How wonderful that was!

One day, Kathi was over visiting with her baby. I was enjoying holding my precious, wiggly grandson. Smiling, I looked at her and said, "Why don't you and Bob go out sometime so I can babysit Jeremy?"

She looked at me, surprised. "You always told us kids you wouldn't babysit for us!"

I held my sweet grandson closer. "I meant not all the time. I'll babysit when I want to."

After that, she and Bob took advantage of my offer and started going out occasionally, after checking with me first.

My life seemed full now, but my nursing dream remained in the back of my mind.

By the Grace of God.

In the fall of 1974, I enrolled to start part-time in the spring pre-nursing classes at WSU that would begin in January. I was just shy of forty-four years of age, but my age never really worried me.

One mid-December morning, I was working at Susan's store, getting things ready to open for the day. Bill was at work.

I got a phone call from him, saying he had chest pains. "I just thought you'd want to know."

Pulse racing in alarm, I yelled into the phone, "Call an ambulance!"

Of course, he wouldn't and didn't want me to call one.

Ignoring his attitude, I called Susan and hurriedly drove several miles to pick him up at work to take him to the hospital. All the time, worried but praying for the best. This stubborn man was the love of my life, the father of my children. I wasn't ready to live without him.

To our great relief, Bill didn't require surgery. But they kept him in the hospital for about two weeks for assessment, to monitor his high blood pressure, and adjust his new medications. Determined to be by his side, I quit working and spent much of my time with him at the hospital. That was when he found out nurses do much more than "empty bedpans."

By the grace of God, many prayers, wonderful doctors, and great nurses, Bill recovered well. They dismissed him from the hospital on Christmas morning. Our family celebrated Christmas like never before. We were all thankful to have him still with us.

Back to My Dream.

Recovered, Bill went back to work after New Year's Day. Our kids were all grown up, as I had been waiting for when I first thought about going to college. They sometimes spent evenings and Sunday dinners at our house. And we had our grandkids to enjoy. All was going well with everyone. I decided maybe now I could go back to my dream of becoming a nurse.

So, I started my pre-nursing classes at WSU in January, after all.

I could have gone back to work since Bill had recovered but attempting to work to pay my way would be difficult. It would take longer to finish college. And when I started the nursing program, I would not have time to work and study as much as I needed.

I found I could get a student loan and pay it off in small interest-free payments after graduation. At $12 a credit hour, the total loan would only be about $7,000. This seemed like a good plan, so I signed up for the loan. I also completely stopped the sewing business that I had been doing occasionally to start college full time that summer. I could only do so much.

Granny Time

Even though I was back in school, family remained important to me. Charlie, Connie, and little four-year-old Tracy lived in the house next door now. Sometimes when I came home in the afternoon from my classes, Tracy, hearing my car, would look out of her bedroom window. She was supposed to be napping.

As I drove up and stopped my car, she'd wave madly and holler out the window at me. "Granny, do you gotta study?" She knew if I had to study, she couldn't come over then.

Sometimes, even if I needed to study, I couldn't resist the temptation. I'd smile and call back, "No. Come on over. Ask Mommy first." That Granny Time was very important to me, to us both.

"Super Plus" Paper.

That summer, I took a required sociology class. The first assignment from the professor was a two-page autobiography. I went to him and asked with a grin, "Could I have four pages? Since I'm twice as old as most of the other students."

He looked at me with a whimsical smile. "Sure!"

I had never thought about writing an autobiography. It was the days of talking about women's lib. Some students talked and wrote about becoming liberated. But I did my long paper in non-rhyming poetry form and titled it "Living." I wrote about my life from the time I could remember as a child until when I was forty-five years old. (The poem is at the end of this book.)

I wrote about my childhood with my many siblings, meeting Bill at sixteen and falling in love. I wrote about getting married at eighteen and growing our family. In the end, I stated, "Bill and me, life is good: most of it is still ahead of us."

When the paper came back, the professor had written on it, "Super Plus!" And after a lot of hard work, I earned an "A" in the class.

Later that summer, I showed our kids my sociology paper, "Living." They shared it, excited to learn things about my childhood they hadn't known. But I didn't show the paper to Bill, not feeling he would be interested and might think it was silly. Part of my reasoning was because if our kids and I started talking about my paper and my going to college, he would leave the house. He'd go out to the garage and find something to do there. I admit, it hurt my feelings a little.

Then he surprised me again.

One Sunday evening in late August, our kids and their families had all gone home after another get-together. Bill and I sat at the dining table snacking on leftovers. He looked at me and, in his typical quiet way, asked, "What is that story our kids are talkin' about?"

The paper was in a trifold. I laid it on the table beside him. I never saw him read it, but later I saw it in a slot in his secretary desk. He never mentioned reading the poem, and I never asked him about it.

Bill's secretary desk

Always Need Bill.

About two weeks into the fall classes, Bill caught me off guard again, asking, "What are you taking this semester?"

I was stunned speechless for a moment. When I recovered, I told him about my classes. After that conversation, he often asked me how things were going at school. He began encouraging me throughout the rest of nursing, and yes, the rest of our life together.

Several of my later classes in pre-nursing were in the behavioral sciences. I believed that Bill's earlier reaction may have been because he thought I would leave him when I finished nursing school. That maybe he thought I wouldn't need him anymore. After he read my "Living" poem, I think he realized I wasn't planning to do that.

Later, I was talking with my brother Bob one day. I told him what I believed Bill had been thinking and said, "Bill couldn't get rid of me if he tried!"

Smiling, Bob said in teasing, "He may have tried a few times."

Like many couples, Bill and I had some difficult times through the years, but we always worked through them. I would always need him, always love him.

Chapter Two
TRIALS OF LIFE

People Your Age.

That fall I enrolled in a religion class because I wanted to know more about different beliefs. I thought it would be helpful in my nursing practice and my life.

The young instructor assigned his students to do a paper summarizing the world's religions. We worked long and diligently on the papers, as much of the information was unfamiliar to us. Then we submitted our papers for grading.

I soon had my first negative experience with age discrimination in college.

When I received my paper back, he'd marked it with a "C." There were no comments about why I had that grade. I went to the instructor and asked him about it, wanting an explanation.

He looked at me. "Well, people your age—" He abruptly stopped speaking, took my paper, marked out the "C," and wrote "A" in its place. Then he took out his grade book and changed the grade there, too. Still no explanation. I didn't believe he had read my paper, which was frustrating.

As our study groups worked together, I did well on other papers and tests. At the end of the class, I made an "A." If I had not stood up to the instructor, I believe I would have gotten a lower grade in the class. This was the first of other similar situations I later dealt with in my college career.

Generally, though, I was just one of the group of students.

Besides that class, it was challenging to keep my grades up. Struggling with math, I took a non-credit remedial algebra class. It helped to lessen my tension concerning math. I made the honor roll, which I was determined to do if possible. Bill's encouragement was a tremendous help.

Contentment at Home.

Because I wanted to, I continued doing the cooking and housework. I was determined to have a semi-normal life and take my classes at the same time. We also welcomed our kids and grandkids to our home every chance we got. Sometimes, we had guests visiting on weekends, which Bill and I both enjoyed. Our home was known as "Willie's Hotel."

At the time, 1975, we had lived there on Grove Street for seventeen years. Having restored the house, we kept it in top-notch appearance and condition. I planted lots of much-admired flowers in both front and back yards. We had no intention of ever moving. Then....

Housing Problems.

After beginning the fall semester, we started hearing rumors and news reports about the city of Wichita's plans to build an urban highway on the east side of Grove Street. The road would start several blocks south of our house and continue north for many blocks. Unfortunately, our house was smack-dab in the middle of the highway plans.

1976 Grove Street house

We were devastated, but we had no choice but to move. Our kids had spent their formative years and grown up in this home. Frustrated with the problem, I investigated the possibility of having the house moved. It would be expensive, if we could move it at all.

Bill firmly said, "Absolutely not!"

We would receive top market value for our house and be well compensated to relocate. Still, it was upsetting.

As we started looking for another house, I told myself we were just moving our home to a different place. It wasn't easy to accept that.

I hoped to find another nice, older, possibly Victorian house that our collection of Victorian furniture would fit into. Bill wasn't that interested.

We looked at many newer houses for sale and some older ones in mid-town and in Wichita's historic district. I found a registered landmark two-story, large brick house on

Park Place, built in 1875. However, it needed some—yes, a lot of—restoration. Despite that, it strongly appealed to me.

Bill wasn't as enamored with it, but said, "If that house is what you want, okay. Don't expect me to do the work on it." I know he hoped that would change my mind. It didn't.

Before we could get our settlement from the city for the house on Grove Street, they sold this Victorian house to an older couple. I was very disappointed.

Sometimes You Settle.

Continuing our search, we located a smaller one-and-a-half-story brick house, built in 1915 in the College Hill Division. We signed a contract. After receiving our settlement and relocation money the following late spring, we purchased the house and moved into it.

Most of the neighborhood's houses were built in the "horse and buggy days." Few people had cars. Streets were still not paved and neighbors often shared driveways. Our driveway was on the property line, so we shared it with our neighbor, a friendly elderly widow.

Because of the shared driveway, we couldn't park there. Bill disliked this situation. If a visitor parked there, it would prevent our neighbor from coming in or going out. A couple of times, she came to our front door and asked someone to move. The visitor had to move their car and then park in front of our house on the street. It also concerned Bill about the problem when he wasn't there.

1976 Belmont house

Another issue was the difficulty we had in fitting our massive Victorian furniture into this house. We managed most of the treasured pieces, and I tried to accept the change. Having the familiar furniture I had collected around me helped a lot. And I took comfort with planting my favorite flowers in the yard.

Even though the house wasn't my dream one, Bill and I settled into the new home and began liking it. We also continued our family trips to the lake on Sunday afternoons throughout the summer and into the fall.

"You'll make the cut."

With the coming of spring, it was time for pre-nursing students to apply for admission to the nursing program.

They required us to pass an admission exam, where our grade point average counted. I was hopeful because of my good pre-nursing grades.

But they placed some of my fellow students and me on the alternate waiting list. I was understandably disappointed, even devastated. Yet, there was the possibility they could still admit me because of how the admission process was designed.

I was tearful and reluctant to tell Bill what had happened. When I did, he encouraged me to be patient. "Don't worry, you'll make the cut," he told me in comfort.

One evening after work, he brought me a surprise. He'd bought me an expensive nurse's watch with a second hand. Sometimes he was a quiet spoken man, but always he supported me.

Being placed on the alternate list didn't mean we had failed the exam. If I had failed it, I would have to take classes to improve my test scores and grades and apply again for admission in a year. Or I could quit, not an option for me.

WSU only admitted a set number of students to the nursing degree program each year. Over twice that many applied. Some applicants had attended pre-nursing classes at other colleges, including Kansas State University and the University of Kansas, hoping to be accepted in one of them. Some were accepted into more than one school, so they chose to go to another school besides WSU.

Within a few days, most of us on the alternate list were notified they accepted us into the WSU College of Health Professions for the BSN. What a day! Now all I had to do was finish my degree.

Our Toys.

Bill enjoyed looking at ads in the paper for used cars, campers, and boats. He always kept our family in good used cars and "toys." Soon after we moved to Wichita, he purchased a used paddle boat but before long traded it up to a small motorboat. Then he bought a nice, small used camper. He usually found bargains and made several upgrades of boats and campers.

Well into the fall semester of 1976, I came home one afternoon, and Bill had traded our boat and camper for a cabin cruiser. The cabin on the boat had a kitchenette and a full-sized bed, so we could spend the night in it. The boat was small but still powerful enough to pull water skiers. It seemed odd to me to have our boat and camper together as one item.

Not a Sissy

Even though it was late October and cool, Bill was eager to take us—John, Charlie, and me—waterskiing. We went to Cheney Lake, a smaller lake that would not be so cold. But he really wanted to try his new boat on a bigger lake.

It was exciting to launch our cabin cruiser that first time. We all enjoyed riding around for a while getting used to the new boat. We didn't mind the cool air blowing over us.

Finally, Bill asked, "Who wants to go skiing first?"

I had never swum in frigid water, as my brothers had sometimes done on the farm. But I was eager anyway. I figured the guys would want to be polite and "let the ladies" (me) go first, so I volunteered.

I threw the skis into the water, climbed down the side ladder, and jumped into the lake. I sucked in a breath of shock. For a moment, the cold water nearly paralyzed me. I was determined not to complain and managed to get up on the skis. Out of the water, the air was much warmer, so I skied and skied and skied, not wanting to get back into the water.

When I couldn't hold on any longer, I turned loose of the ski rope. Yes, the water was still just as cold and, again, stole my breath.

Bill circled around, and I eagerly climbed back into the boat. I did my best not to shiver because I didn't want the guys to think I was a "sissy." I said little about the cold water.

"You guys are crazy!"

Charlie decided to go next. He climbed down the ladder, jumped into the water—didn't complain, but may have flinched—and skied for a long time, as I did. When he got out of the water, he barely commented about how cold the water was, and he did shiver a bit.

Now it was John's turn. He climbed part-way down the ladder, jumped into the water, and sank out of sight for a moment. He shot straight up out of the water. Grabbing the ladder, he used a few words that were not repeatable here.

As he climbed back into the boat, he yelled at Charlie and me. "You guys are crazy!" He may have been right, but we still had fun.

Rocking with the Waves

If nothing else, the first experience on Bill's cabin cruiser was a memorable one. For several years, we had many more pleasant trips and cruises with our family. Occasionally someone mentioned that first frigid waterskiing incident and we laughed about it.

Beyond those times with others, Bill and I often spent lovely nights anchored in our cozy cruiser, at the water's edge, rocking with the waves.

Life Changes Again.

Our life seemed always to be complex, what with keeping up with our family, my classes, and Bill's job. The owner of the company where Bill had worked for many years decided to retire. He sold the business to a company back east. Bill's position changed and his pay decreased. So, he started searching the ads for another job.

J.I. Case had started a new division of their trucking business in Wichita and was hiring five new truck drivers. As Bill and I talked about the job, he said, "I don't know whether they would hire someone my age." He was fifty-three years old. It was a union job, and the increase in pay and benefits would be huge.

I said, "You won't know unless you apply." I always tried to be positive.

Bill had driven over one million miles and never had a ticket or a moving violation. He applied, and they chose him "First Driver" over fifty other applicants. I was proud of him.

He would drive a tractor-trailer and haul heavy equipment.

As First Driver, he called each weekend to choose the run he wanted of the available weekly runs. He was usually home three days each week. Sometimes he selected a longer run to go to places he wanted to see. Since he was home for three—sometimes four—days a week, we spent more time together than many couples.

Our plans were going well. Bill was home for the Thanksgiving and Christmas holidays, and our family celebrated them in our usual festive ways. Every year seemed to get better, especially with having our grandkids.

I had just one more semester to go before graduation with my BSN in nursing, fulfilling another step toward my dream of being a nurse.

1978 Grandkids at Christmas

1978 Christmas with grandkids

I began that last semester, and the classes were difficult and challenging. I was giving full-time and more to my studies, determined to do my best. Bill and my family understood the pressure I was under and always stood by to support me in any way I needed.

Bill was content in his new job and enjoying the freedom of being out of the office, driving on the road alone.

Out of the Blue.

One afternoon, I was home studying while Bill was at work. The phone rang, and I answered it. The realtor who showed us our house and assisted us in buying it was calling. He had also shown us the old Victorian house on Park Place. He knew it was my first choice, and that it disappointed me when it sold before we could buy it.

After a brief greeting, he told me the house on Park Place was on the market again. The older couple who had bought it soon realized the cost of restoring the house would be more than they wanted to spend. They listed the house and started looking for a smaller, newer one. My heart raced with excitement.

Park Place house

I convinced myself we had a good reason for selling our current house. Bill had never liked the shared driveway, being more concerned about that issue now that he was gone so much of the time. It would always be a problem. Besides that, he wanted a driveway where he could sometimes park his car, camper, or his boat.

What would Bill think about moving again? He was on the road when I got the phone call, so I thought about the situation. When he came home, I let him get settled down and comfortable. As we sat and ate our meal, I calmly told him about the realtor's call concerning the house on Park Place.

Bill seemed astonished, even stunned. But he knew from the time I saw the old house how much I wanted it. He looked straight at me and firmly said, "I thought you liked this house. Why would you want to move into that old run-down house?"

Hoping it would make a difference in how he felt, I reminded him of the problems with our shared driveway. And I reminded him about the two-car garage, which we needed. The garage had replaced the original barn on the former small 1875 farm. As more enticement, I mentioned the small garden plot at the back of the lot. But Bill was still not fully convinced.

Mostly, I couldn't forget the house with the stained-glass windows in every room except the "maid's room." Plus, there was the cathedral double front door and four fireplaces. I didn't pursue the situation any more then.

Added Temptation.

Still thinking of the possibility of buying the registered landmark house, I became concerned the final price would be more than our current house and out of our financial range. I talked with the realtor about it. He told me about a low interest registered landmark loan which would be available for the house in any amount. I started thinking even more.

Ever since we moved to Wichita those many years ago, Bill looked at ads in the paper for used cars. He would also mention seeing ads for small airplanes. Over the years, he continued to be aware of the prices for them. One evening, he mentioned seeing a Cessna 150 for sale for $6,000. But the seller wanted cash, and we had not built up a savings account after I started nursing school. The plane had been in the ads for some time. How did that figure into my plans?

The realtor determined, even after his fee, we would

come out about even between the price of our houses. We could still get the low-interest loan on the house and Bill would have the extra money he needed to buy the airplane he wanted. Neither of us could fly, but we could both learn. And this was one of my childhood dreams: flying in a plane.

The next time Bill came home from a road trip, I hesitantly told him about the opportunity of getting the special loan and having the money for the plane as well. He listened intently but said nothing.

Making Me Happy.

Bill had been home a couple of days. One evening, he was sitting in his captain's chair at our dining table, and I sat close by. We had just finished our meal. He looked at me and spoke quietly. "If buying that house is what it takes to make you happy, we'll buy it. But don't expect me to do the work on it."

I tried not to leap out of my chair. Instead, I hurried to him, hugged him, and assured him I would take care of the work, one way or another. Hard work never bothered me.

This wonderful man that I loved so much always wanted me to have what I wanted whenever possible. But how was this possible? He was away for over half the time. I was struggling to finish my last semester in nursing school. Yet, all my life I have always, or usually, been able to work things out to do what I wanted to do, sometimes with a lot of help.

A few days later, when Bill was home, the realtor came by with the completed contract for our new house on Park Place. He had arranged the low-interest loan for us so Bill could also buy the Cessna 150. And the realtor sold our current house for our asking price. The buyers were willing to wait until we could move, and Bill bought the airplane.

Cessna 150

It was a stressful time. The plans to move were up to me, since Bill was gone much of the time, and I was still going full-time to college. I made a plan. I contacted the movers ahead of time and got boxes to pack the kitchen items, our clothing and anything else I could box up. Our kids were a tremendous help.

As soon as we had possession of our new house, the movers hauled everything there and placed the furniture where I wanted it. We had the Steinway grand piano moved by special movers. Bill moved the cabin cruiser himself.

We were completely moved before spring break, for which I was thankful. I was able to keep up my nursing schoolwork, but the break was a welcome relief. It gave me a chance to relax for a few days and enjoy being outside. Still, there was a task that couldn't wait.

Battling the Hedge.

There was a tall country hedge growing across the front of our double corner lot. The hedge continued down the side from the corner of the yard to the alley. I think it was over one-hundred-fifty feet of eight-foot hedge. The roots were causing cracks in the retaining wall on both sides of the yard.

The ugly hedge was not original to the house, probably planted many decades after they built the house. I didn't want it there. This break time was the only chance I would have to remove the hedge.

Bill left on his weekly run over the road, so I had my chance to dive into this project. I rented a power saw and started cutting the hedge close to the ground. Not a simple job. Most of the trunks were eight inches across, or more. As I cut each one off, I dragged it to the back of our yard. It took me two days to saw the bushes down and two big trucks to haul the mess off.

When Bill came home, he was surprised... yet not too much. He knew how independent and determined I could be sometimes.

I wanted to remove the stumps before sprouts started growing and become a bigger nuisance than the hedge. After they were gone, I wanted to plant flowers there.

So, I rented a stump puller. I quickly discovered that it took more strength than I could muster. Only a little discouraged, I returned it and would try something else.

I had heard about using saltpeter granules to kill plant growth. This sounded good to me. I used Bill's electric drill to drill several deep holes in each stump, a time-consuming job. Then I filled the holes with the granules and waited to see if the process worked. It did.

My problem was only partially solved. The stumps dried but couldn't be removed for over a year.

Undeterred by the inconvenience, I planted peonies and antique roses around the stumps. The roses bloomed beautifully that summer and smelled so good. As the stumps could gradually be pulled, I planted more flowers where they had been. In a couple of years, there were over sixty peony bushes and over one-hundred antique rose bushes. I also planted other favorite flowers, iris and tulips.

Restoration Challenges

Bill had many reasons he did not want to buy the Park Place house. I'm not sure the ugly hedge had bothered him as much as it did me. He was more against the outside appearance.

A doctor and his wife in 1915 bought the house built in 1875. She immediately modernized it for those times. Because it was a Victorian style, I knew it would have had ornate porch posts, handrails, and turnings. But they were gone now. The wife had the fancy architectural elements replaced with square posts and turnings.

A few years later, she had the front and south side of the beautiful brick walls painted barn red. She told her family she wanted to cover the aging appearance of the bricks. I disliked that "improvement." My plan was to strip the red paint from the walls before we moved into the house.

I located and contacted some of her descendants. They were friendly and appreciated that we were restoring the old house. Older descendants remembered the elaborate porches and gave me family pictures that showed the original turnings. I wanted to restore them to what they were like originally.

Soon after moving there, I subscribed to The Old House Journal. One issue had a picture of a large, octagonal gazebo with handrails, a side stairway, and a balcony with railings. That gazebo was a long-standing landmark with a mansion back east.

Because our house was a registered historic landmark, we could only do what might have been correct for the time. There was an empty space on our double lot at the back, perfect for a gazebo. When I showed the picture to Bill and told him what I wanted to do, he just looked at me in resignation. He knew I would somehow have one.

There were so many things to be done at the same time. I talked with a local contractor carpenter well known for remodeling and restoring old houses. Showing him the gazebo pictures and the original porch turnings, he was immediately interested.

The contractor often worked with a local woodworking craftsman. The two men discussed the project and were excited to take it on. They used the pictures I provided to plan what was needed. The craftsman would make the desired woodwork. The contractor would then build the gazebo and restore the porch turnings to the original appearance.

I had not stripped the brick wall as I had hoped to do before moving into the house. But that summer I was now ready for that task.

I Never Give Up.

The side of the house was two stories tall. I rented industrial scaffolding from a local lumberyard, which they loaded into the pickup for me. The scaffolding framework was so heavy it was difficult for me to handle, but I did.

After setting up the first section, I lifted heavy wooden planks in place to stand on. I tied a rope to the second section of scaffolding and I pulled it up and set it in place. Eventually, I had a structure twelve feet high, with planks to stand on and rails around the sides for safety. It was a struggle for someone only five feet tall.

Now I was ready to strip the bricks by using what was advertised as one of the "best paint removers on the market." I quickly discovered that the old paint, baked on by the sun for decades, would not budge. Not willing to give up, I resorted to my own tried-and-true paint stripper. It was something I had made and used for many years to refinish antiques.

I added a cup of flour to a two-gallon bucket of cold water and stirred it well. I added a can of lye to the mixture. The lye heated the mixture, cooking it. When it cooled, the mixture became a thick paste.

I brushed the paste on a large section of several square feet, then let it sit for a half hour. Using a fine steel brush and spraying with a water hose, I scrubbed the section of bricks. All the old paint was removed. I was very pleased that the bricks looked so much nicer.

When I had stripped a six-feet wide by four-feet high area, I moved the scaffolding down to the next level. This was not an easy task for a woman my size. I did one area each day and continued working down to the lowest level. Then I, again, had to move the scaffolding and set it up once more to do the next strip.

The paint stripping took several weeks to finish because I did it in the morning, two or three days a week. I didn't work on the scaffolding when Bill was home. I didn't want him to see me climbing and worry. I'm sure he did, but he never said anything.

About the time I finished the slow-going job, the contractor and the craftsman were ready with the woodwork for the porches and gazebo. The contractor removed the porch posts and replaced them with the exact replicas of the original ones.

My Brother's Help.

My oldest brother, Don, had learned carpentry from Daddy. Don worked as a carpenter, building houses before moving to Wichita to work in the aircraft industry. He was now retired. I told him what I was going to have done, and he said he would like to help with the project. I was pleased to let him.

The contractor was fine with having Don replace the handrails with their many small turnings. He worked about three hours each morning before it got too hot, four days each week. We ate lunch together and visited about old times. I was glad to have the chance to get to know him again.

The contractor and crew focused full time on the gazebo. It took several weeks to finish the project. They poured a ten-foot octagonal concrete floor and set eight posts in place by building the framework. The gazebo had handrails all around except in the entry. Then they laid the floor for the balcony and set eight short-side posts to the handrails in place. After adding the stairway up to the balcony, it was complete. They painted the porch trim and gazebo white, the original color. I was very pleased with it all.

Gazebo at Park Place house

A Magical Dance

The gazebo caught the attention of pedestrians walking by and drivers as well. Something especially attracted one couple.

One afternoon, someone knocked on our kitchen door. I opened it in surprise to find a young man standing there with a young woman. He said, "This is my wife and our wedding anniversary. We were wondering if we could go up on the balcony of your gazebo. We would like to play music on our battery radio and dance."

Pleased to help them, I said, "Yes! Sure!"

About sundown, I heard music and saw the couple

dancing there on the gazebo's balcony. They danced and stayed there for a couple of hours, with the corner streetlight casting a special glow on them. It was almost magical, romantic.

Chapter Three
LIVING MY DREAM

Graduation Focus.

It was time I paid full attention to my classes and upcoming graduation. Life had certainly become complicated with the move and keeping up with my family. But I managed to keep my grades up and made the honor roll. Being one of the older students hadn't mattered at all. As I had done all my life, I focused on what I wanted to do, and did it.

My kids were proud of me, enthusiastic and excited for what I had accomplished. Bill, always quiet, didn't say much. Yet I could tell he was openly pleased.

May 1979, there were thousands of bachelors' graduates in many areas of study at WSU. Due to so many students, the graduation ceremony did not acknowledge each student. The nursing department, however, had a special pinning ceremony for nearly one hundred graduates. We nursing students chose to attend only this event.

The ceremony was open to family members and other guests of the students. I was so glad it was held on Saturday and Bill could be there for my big moment. Our kids, grandkids, and some of my siblings were excited to be among the several hundred guests.

We all gathered in the large room with the graduates sitting together in rows facing the front. The guests sat in rows behind us. One of the professors welcomed the guests and asked the parents to stand. Everyone applauded.

Then she asked the husbands and wives of the graduates to stand for recognition, to more applause. Our kids later told me that as soon as the professor said "husbands," Bill stood up before anyone else, unusual for him. He stood for the applause.

After congratulating the students, the professor had each of us walk to the front where she pinned on our well-earned nursing pin. More applause followed before we all joined with our families and guests, visiting with everyone for a while.

When our kids, their families, and my siblings gathered at our house afterward for a "reception," I discovered another surprise from my husband. Bill had secretly arranged for refreshments for us. It was a very special moment in my life.

Red Cadillac Trip.

After completing nursing school, we still had to take and pass a test by the Kansas State Board of Nursing for our license before we could practice as a nurse. Back then, graduates had to go to Topeka to take the sit-down paper test. Now, the tests are taken by computer, without having to travel to Topeka.

We heard stories from former graduates (grads) about how they usually tried to make the process a fun and festive happening. The exams were on Saturday morning. Many of the grads drove to Topeka the day before and stayed in hotels. They would go out to dinner at nightclubs where they could wine, dine, and dance into the night. Sometimes they overindulged and needed supervision getting back to their rooms.

That's where I came in. My classmates knew I didn't drink. I hadn't gone out drinking with them during nursing school. As we planned our trip, we arranged for one non-drinker to be with several grads.

I was going to take a deluxe 1972 red Cadillac sedan that Bill had reconditioned. It had a white top and white leather upholstery. I had no trouble finding five of my young classmates to ride with me. We met at a designated place on campus after lunch, then headed to Topeka. Everyone was excited.

We checked into our motel by mid-afternoon. It took a while for the six of us to get settled into our three rooms. Late afternoon, we loaded back into the Cadillac. The "girls"—all in their twenties—and I decided to go eat fast food for now.

Our Wild Muppets Night.

After eating, it was close to sundown and the girls wanted to ride around in the Cadillac before going to the clubs for the night. As I slowly drove down the street, they rolled down the windows and started waving and hollering at people we passed by. Many of them waved and yelled back.

A couple of the girls stuck their heads out the windows. Then they pulled themselves up and sat on the edge of the window frame. They laughed, waved, and hollered even more at anyone who looked their way.

Old enough to know better and worried about them, I pulled over and parked. I told them to get back in the car, not willing to drive again until they did. When they did as requested, I went back to cruising along. I swear the girls had not had anything to drink. They were just excited.

As we continued along the main street in mid-town, we noticed the large sign advertising the "movie of the year" The Muppets, featuring Miss Piggy.

Someone yelled, "Let's go to the Muppet movie!" Soon they were all in agreement to see the movie and forget going to the nightclub. I was also in agreement.

I got us to the theater early and we got the best seats. We loaded up on popcorn, snacks, and soft drinks. When the movie ended, everyone was still too excited to go back to the hotel. So, we watched it again. Quite a wild evening.

Finally, we loaded back into my Cadillac and returned to our motel. We found some of our classmates staggering along with the help of sober fellow grads. I was pleased that wasn't us.

Waiting for Results.

Exhausted after our busy day and night of movie watching, we got a much-needed night's sleep. After a good breakfast and getting serious again, we went to take the test for our nursing license.

It had been nice to be distracted the day before, but I was worried about the test. I was confident but concerned.

Relieved when it was done, our much more subdued group stopped for a fast-food lunch before heading home. We wouldn't get the test results for several weeks.

My Dream Comes True.

It was good to be back home, but the waiting for the result was difficult. Until we received our Kansas license to practice as a Registered Nurse, we were allowed to work in hospitals, as we did as undergraduates. The pay was not good, but the experience was helpful.

I worked second shift—which I preferred—in a local hospital on the Psychiatric Unit. When I received my license, I was soon promoted to Charge Nurse of the unit. The pay was better, but as is common in nursing, I had to work every other weekend. Bill was only home on long weekends, but we tried to make the most of our time together.

I heard about a new staffing plan in another hospital in Wichita. The plan consisted of positions for eight licensed On-Call nurses. I decided to check it out because the nurses could work full-time or part-time as they wished. And they didn't have to work weekends. The nurse also wouldn't know which nursing unit they would be needed in until they reported for duty. I was okay with that.

It pleased me to be offered one of the positions. I gave my two weeks' notice and accepted the new job. But first, I decided to take some much-needed time off to be with Bill.

Bill and Me Time.

We loved our family and enjoyed spending time with them whenever we could. One or more of our grandkids often spent nights with us. And we shared a lot of pleasant Sunday afternoons together at the lake. We also took many wonderful trips to visit Bill's family in Missouri and to my brother's ranch in Colorado. The one thing we hadn't had was some "Bill and Me" time. Ever since starting our family we hadn't taken a vacation alone.

Bill and I decided to take a week-long vacation before starting my new job. We had taken weekend trips to Grand Lake in Oklahoma with our family and liked the lake and its accommodations, so that's where we went.

We had our cabin cruiser with its kitchenette and a bed where we could spend our nights. But I suggested—yes, insisted—we rent a cabin for the week. Bill gladly agreed. I also told him I didn't want to spend time cooking and would rather go to the café close to our cabin.

After going to the café the first morning, I decided I didn't like having to get dressed so early. Bill was the early riser and came to my rescue, as always. He stocked our cabin's kitchen with food. We had cereal for breakfast and sandwiches for lunch in our place. Then we got dressed up in the evening to eat out.

We cruised around the lake in the afternoon, relaxing and enjoying the peace and quiet. A rare thing in our busy lives. Bill also tried fishing, with little luck.

Bonnie in cabin cruiser

Skinny dippin'.

It was fall, but I still wanted to waterski, and Bill was happy to let me. The water was warm and smooth. I tossed the skis into the water and got on them. To my delight, Bill pulled me around the lake for over an hour. He would smile back at me, watching for my signal to stop.

When I finally did, he pulled the boat over to the edge of the lake and turned off the engine. I handed up the skis and continued swimming around in the warm water. I thought about how my brothers used to go skinny dipping on the farm when I was a little girl. I'd never done that. Was this my chance to try it?

I looked around. There didn't seem to be anyone else in the area.

Excited and feeling daring, I stripped off my bathing suit while in the shoulder-deep water. As Bill looked at me and smiled, I tossed the suit up to him. He just grinned some more.

I floated, swam, and splashed around. Now I knew why my brothers liked skinny dippin'!

After a while my curiosity was satisfied and I asked Bill to throw me a towel. Still grinning, he did. I walked out of the water, wrapped in the towel, and climbed up the boat ladder straight into Bill's open arms. I expected us to head back to our cabin where we would dress and go out to dinner.

Bill had other ideas. He was always prepared for any situation. He'd already stocked the kitchenette with food. He asked me if I would like him to anchor the cruiser and spend the night on the lake. I eagerly agreed.

By that time, the sun had gone down, and it was dark outside. Bill put together enough snacks to make us a delicious meal and we ate in the dim cabin lights. It had been a long, exciting day. We fell asleep snuggled in bed, rocking with the gentle waves.

The next morning, we went back to the cabin to eat breakfast and lunch there. The remaining vacation days were spent relaxing, fishing, skiing some more, and dining at the café in the evenings.

We had other vacations at Grand Lake, but none compared to that one alone with Bill when I got a little daring. There were no other skinny-dippin' times.

New Job and Flying Time.

When our vacation was over, I reported to the office of the On-Call Nursing Program. There were usually several units with a staffing shortage. I could choose where I wanted to work. I had not decided yet on a specific area of practice because I wanted to try them all.

I could usually choose to work in Oncology or Intensive Care, including the Newborn Intensive Care unit. Over time I worked in most of the hospital units, except Labor-Delivery and Surgery. Often the Charge Nurse of a unit would request my supervisor to send me to their unit, something I was proud of.

After several months, I became one of the best-known nurses in the hospital. Sometimes a Charge Nurse of a unit where I wasn't working would invite me to their unit during my lunch time for a potluck meal they were having. That always made me feel good.

There was an option to work any shift, including twelve-hour shifts from 7 a.m. to 7 p.m. or 7 p.m. to 7 a.m. Occasionally I worked the day shift but didn't really like the night shift.

One time in a snowstorm, we were held over into the next twelve-hour shift because our replacements could not get there. And we could not get home, either. We took turns, trying to take two-hour naps, mostly without success. That was the worst staffing experience of my nursing career.

About the time I changed hospitals to work in their On-Call Nursing Program, I started taking flying lessons. One step toward reaching another of my childhood dreams.

A Favorite Room.

The previous owners of our house on Park Place installed a much-needed modern kitchen in the short time they were there. We appreciated that. The old kitchen had not been updated for decades. We were so pleased with the beautiful new cabinets and the new kitchen layout.

There was a nice-sized double sink in the middle of the cabinets on the inside wall. The refrigerator sat at one end by the door into the laundry room, where we kept our freezer.

They had created a center island with cabinets that extended from the outer wall into the middle of the room. That was a great place for preparations and storage. Overhead cabinets were a helpful addition, too. We also liked the new electric inset stovetop and the electric oven set into the side of the cabinets.

Other improvements were the beautiful, light-colored wall paneling and natural wood-plank floors. Thankfully, they kept the original beveled glass kitchen side door that opened onto the back porch.

To help with warmth, a small wood-burning heating stove sat between the island and the side of the room. We had space for a little dinette table and two chairs in front of a side window that overlooked the back porch.

When Bill was home, I cooked his favorite foods in cold weather, and he would start a fire in that little stove. Then, we'd eat our meals or snacks at the small table, enjoying time to discuss our jobs, our family, and making plans for future vacations. And, yes, we often talked about my flying lessons.

Bill usually kept his harmonica close by and liked playing it as I sang along. He would encourage me to play along with my guitar. This kitchen was the coziest place in the whole house, and that first winter, we spent most of our time there.

Bill with his harmonica.

Eventually, we would retire to our upstairs master bedroom with its grand fireplace. I always enjoyed it when Bill would light a fire there, especially when it was cold outside.

It didn't take him too long to start liking our new home. Soon, friends and relatives visited us on most weekends, enjoying coming to what Bill considered his new "Willie's Hotel."

Another House Remodel Project.

As the weather became cold, I couldn't work in the yard and wasn't flying as often. Now I had the time to redo the wallpaper in our home. Something I had done many times over the years and so wasn't afraid of tackling the big job. When I was twelve years old and my family lived in Winchester, Kansas, I learned how to paper stairways. Mom hired paper hangers to paper the spiral staircase in our Victorian house. I sat close by watching them for two exciting days.

The paper here was nearly new, but not my choice of patterns. I didn't feel it went with the many stained-glass windows in every room except the kitchen and maid's room.

The wallpaper store in our historic neighborhood had reproduction paper in Victorian era styles. Many of the beautiful designs would blend well with those windows. I spent hours looking at pattern books and taking samples home before I finally decided on the perfect patterns.

My first task was to paper the two-story side wall by the stairway. It was like the stair-wall I had papered in our first house, except this wall was about two feet higher than in the other house. This time, little Charlie wasn't there to pray for me as he had done with the first project.

A Few Anxious Moments.

There was a landing halfway up on the stairway, which turned to the upper floor. I placed our folding eight-foot stepladder on the landing. The top of the ladder was even with the top of the handrail on the second floor. I laid a one-by-twelve-inch wooden plank, twelve feet long, from the top of the ladder over the lower stairs to the top of the handrail.

I took great care and stood on the wooden plank to paper the side wall. The longest strips of wallpaper were over sixteen feet long, reaching from the second-floor ceiling down to the bottom of the stairway on the first floor.

Without telling Bill ahead of time, I papered the stairway when he was at work. I didn't want to worry him. When he came home and saw the papering done, he didn't say anything for a moment. Then he said, "That looks nice, but you shouldn't have done it. I would have hired someone to paper the wall."

I think he felt he needed to say the words. Although he knew he probably couldn't have stopped me from doing the risky job. By now he knew how determined I could be at times.

The papering task wasn't as dangerous as it sounds. I stood on the plank within inches of the wall and could lean against it for support and to keep my balance. I will admit, though, there were a few anxious moments. And I said a few prayers.

Determined, I papered the upstairs and downstairs halls. I entered the formal front parlor through a large double doorway and papered the ten-foot walls. The same paper design complimented the massive beveled and stained-glass front window in the parlor.

Of course, I had to paper the multi-purpose room with its ten-foot walls, even though the paper there was also fairly new. Just not my preference.

With the rooms we used for our Thanksgiving and Christmas holidays finished, it was time to take a wallpapering break and get ready for time with family and friends. I would resume my plan to redo the back stairway and the four upstairs bedrooms later.

Chapter Four
ENJOYING LIFE

Our Beautiful House.

The parlor was another of our favorite rooms. Our Victorian settee upholstered in a rose sateen brocade sat in front of the large stained-glass side window. The window's colors of red, gold, and blue blended beautifully together. An antique walnut pump organ sat against the wall nearby. The room was also a beautiful setting for our massive Steinway grand piano with its solid rosewood legs, which sat by the inside wall.

The woodwork in our house was showing some aging but looked good in keeping with the age of the house. A decorative, natural wood door at the back of the hall opened into the rest of the house.

Our family and dining room were on the other side of the door. The room was over thirty feet long, extending the width of the house. It was ideal for our holiday and family get-togethers. Both ends of the space had ornate, wood-burning fireplaces inset in bay windows. A beveled framed mirror hung over the mantle of each fireplace. And elaborate stained-glass windows were on each side.

The large, antique dining room furniture I had purchased years ago fit perfectly in the room. With Bill's secretary desk and other familiar antique family furniture, we felt at home. It was perfect when there was a fire lit in the fireplaces.

An open doorway on the other side of the parlor entered a foyer. On one side was the back stairway landing leading up to the maid's room and upstairs hallway. On the other side was a half bath, installed in a former linen closet. The doorway to the kitchen was beyond that.

I loved our new house and was ready to share it with our family for the holidays.

Complicated Holidays.

Bill and I now had four grandkids, two girls and two boys. The oldest was six years old. We realized how much our precious grandkids made the holidays more exciting and meaningful.

Our kids and their families had their own homes and busy lives. Getting us all together for the holidays had become difficult. Dividing the special days between their spouses' families and us wasn't working and stressing everyone out.

We decided the answer was to compromise, celebrate with us on the Sundays before each holiday. The plan worked especially well because Bill was always home on weekends. And as an On-Call Nurse, I could take the weekend off whenever I wanted.

When I chose to, I could work on the holidays. They always needed nurses then, and holiday pay was double the regular pay. While I worked, if Bill was home on the holidays, he could visit with our kids and families in their homes. Or sometimes he traveled to Missouri to visit his family there.

Thanksgiving on Park Place.

We were excited to celebrate our first holiday season in our beautiful Victorian home. The Sunday before Thanksgiving, our family gathered in the dining and family room. Bill had fires burning in the fireplaces to welcome everyone.

The day before, I made good use of our new kitchen, making cookies for our grandkids. I also made pumpkin pies and Bill's favorite apple pies, using the rolling pin he bought me when we were first married.

I got up early Sunday morning to start the yeast dough for hot rolls and cinnamon rolls. In addition, I made gravy, the family's favorite black bean soup, vegetables, and salads. But first, I prepared the twenty-pound turkey and filled it with my much-requested brown rice stuffing. I had made the rice stuffing the first Thanksgiving Bill and I spent together with baby Johnnie.

There were twelve in our family now. We extended the leaves of the dining table so we could all sit together on chairs, stools, and highchairs. We covered the table with a special hand-embroidered tablecloth and topped it with the Fostoria crystal plates I had collected when working estate sales. When we added the cups and goblets for coffee, tea, milk, and juices, the table was nearly full.

As planned, the turkey and all the trimmings were ready by early afternoon and the smells drifted throughout the house, tempting everyone. Because Bill took great pride in carving the turkey, we carried the platter to the head of the table by his plate. The rest of the many, many dishes covered almost every square inch of all available space on the table.

In our family's tradition, we gathered around the table to give thanks to God for all His blessings. This moment was always special to me.

Then all but Bill sat down. He stood with the lighted fireplace behind him and enjoyed his ritual of carving and serving the turkey. With a lot of smiles and eagerness to dive into the meal, we passed the side dishes around. It didn't take long for us to eat until we could eat no more. For now. But we nibbled on leftovers and desserts for the rest of the day.

After Dinner Fun.

Our grandkids got restless once we'd finished the big dinner and tummies were full. So did the rest of us. But it was too cold to go outside.

We opened the door from the dining room into the hallway by the front stairs and parlor. This served as a silent signal for the grandkids to get moving. They ran up the front stairs, through the hallway, down the back stairs, and back into the dining room. Of course, we supervised them. Besides, the adults needed the chance to exercise themselves and used that excuse to run with them.

When the running game calmed down, it was time to move everyone to the parlor. Our kids enjoyed playing the old pump organ and grand piano there. Today, Kathi played the piano, and her siblings joined to sing the hymns they knew so well. I listened wistfully, remembering how they had harmonized together as teenagers. Then they started singing Christmas carols and invited all of us to join in, which I happily did.

Singing around the piano

After our voices wore out, we focused on clearing the table and washing the dishes. Well, almost everyone helped with the tasks. By evening, our families were ready to go home... with lots of leftovers.

We closed the front door after giving the last hugs and kisses to the special people in our lives. Exhausted, Bill and I were ready to relax and enjoy some quiet hours alone. It had been a wonderful time with family, and we had eaten far too much, but we looked forward to doing it all again in a few weeks for Christmas. The alternate day had worked well for us this time, and we planned to make that our new tradition.

Thanksgiving week, having had our family Thanksgiving get-together early, Bill and I had time to relax in the cozy kitchen. That day he played his harmonica, and I played my guitar and sang along to our favorite songs. But sometimes we had our special time together in the family room, settling to watch TV on the sofa, with a warm fire burning bright in the fireplace.

Christmas Preparation.

With Thanksgiving behind us, Christmas was approaching fast. Bill and I went back to work. I was trying to work full time to pay for the gifts I wanted to buy for our family, especially the grandkids. Spoiling the little ones when I could meant a lot to me. And, as always, I had big plans for doing my elaborate Christmas decorations.

With the ten-foot ceilings, I could again have a large Christmas tree as we had on Grove Street for so many years. Bill left on his usual run after Thanksgiving weekend. I took his pickup out to the Christmas tree farm and explained what I wanted. They cut one of the largest trees they had and loaded it for me. Because of the size, I had to leave the tree in the truck bed to wait for Bill's help.

Bill looked at the tree and frowned, but he wasn't surprised. He knew me pretty well by now. Our son, John, helped to carry the massive cedar tree into the front parlor. They built a sturdy stand and set the tree in front of the substantial beveled and stained-glass window, with the tree filling a quarter of the room.

It took me a couple of weeks to decorate the tree, adjusting all the decorations and lights I accumulated over the years. I also decorated throughout the house. The familiar decorations made our new house feel like home to me.

Although Christmas was coming on Wednesday, we gathered early the Sunday morning before, as we had previously done. We piled gifts high under the tree. It delighted the grandkids to see how Santa had already brought gifts for them and put them under our tree early.

Opening Gifts and Not Starving.

Starting with the youngest grandchild, each of them sat on the Victorian sofa to open their gifts as we brought them over. It took over two hours to unwrap the presents. I believe each of the adults enjoyed the gifts others received as much as getting our own. I know I did.

Grandkids on Victorian settee

Christmas dinner was cooking away in the kitchen while we opened gifts. The smells drifting around us of ham, candied sweet potatoes, casseroles and other side dishes made more than one stomach growl in anticipation. There would also be salads, hot rolls, apple pies, cinnamon rolls, and various cookies. We would not starve.

As we had done for the Thanksgiving dinner, we put out my treasured Fostoria crystal plates, cups, and goblets on a colorful Christmas print linen cloth spread over the extended table. A beautiful sight.

When we were ready to eat, Bill carried the large, boneless ham to the table and set it beside his plate. Everyone else carried in the rest of the food, covering most of the table. They placed desserts on the matching antique buffet close by.

Again, as was our family tradition, we prayed for blessings on the food and for our family before we sat down around the table. Then Bill sliced the tender ham and proudly served each of us. It seemed like only a few minutes went by before we all started moaning and groaning once more from eating maybe a bit too much. Some of us chose desserts to eat with our favorite drinks, others waited awhile.

Winding Down.

Our grandkids got restless, and so did the rest of us. The "running game" began again, like at our Thanksgiving dinner. Small feet of excited children pounded throughout the house, up and down stairways and down the upstairs hall. We stayed with them to ensure their safety, also enjoying the chance to move around ourselves.

The grand piano beckoned, so we, again, gathered around it, with Kathi playing for us. We spent most of the afternoon singing favorite Christmas carols and enjoying every moment. Bill, as typical, didn't sing, but he joined in by playing his harmonica.

Off and on during the afternoon, we cleared the table of the many leftovers. We didn't have a dishwasher, so we handwashed the stacks of crystal dishes... and the many pots and pans. As we did so, there was much laughter and a lot of talking about the holidays and our busy lives.

By late afternoon, the energy levels had fallen. Everyone

started collecting their gifts to take home, as well as some leftovers. There was much more food left than Bill and I could ever eat or have room to store.

We wished each of them a Merry Christmas and a wonderful Happy New Year before they left. Then Bill and I were ready for some much-needed relaxing time, sitting on the settee in the family room in front of the flickering fireplace. It didn't take long, though, before we moved to the comfort of our bedroom to settle onto the massive Victorian bed for a good night's sleep.

Surprising Bill's Uncle Carl.

As we had planned, Bill and I drove the next day to Missouri to visit his bachelor uncle Carl to spend Christmas with him. Carl didn't have a phone, so we drove to his house on the farm and surprised him. He wasn't expecting company but was happy to see us.

We brought with us a ham, sweet potatoes, home-canned fruits, and vegetables. It pleased him to see me cooking Christmas dinner on his wood-burning cookstove. He talked about how his sisters, who now lived in the city, grew up cooking on the stove. They hadn't managed the cooking as well as I did, he said. As a child, I had cooked on a similar stove, having the best teacher: Mom.

It was a wonderful day with him on the farm. Bill especially enjoyed it. Growing up close by, he spent many happy Christmases there as a child. But we were ready to head back home the next day.

Getting Back to Normal.

We had a week to relax before New Year's Day, and there were so many things to do. With the holidays over, Bill wanted to get everything back to normal, which meant taking the enormous Christmas tree down. Quite a job.

I stripped off all the prized decorations, and he gladly dragged the tree outside. He took the time to cut the trunk and branches into pieces we could burn in our fireplace. I always enjoyed the special treat of a burning cedar fragrance.

It took me most of the day to gather the decorations spread throughout the house and store them. The task was sad, too. I thought about the good times we had had with our family and looked forward to the next year.

With these tasks done, Bill and I were ready for the new year. We were enjoying our life. His income was more than twice as much as he had ever made. His union health insurance and vacation pay were the best available. And I was enjoying the flexibility of my On-Call Nursing position and being able to have the time I wanted for our family... and time for my flying lessons.

Chapter Five
OTHER DREAMS

Our Guests Favorite Room.

The wonderful holidays were behind us, and winter was coming on strong. It was too cold and blustery to work outside in my yard. Inside the house, the walls were calling me. I needed to get back to papering the four upstairs bedrooms and the back stairway. As before, the wallpaper there was almost new, but not my choice of patterns.

I went back to hanging out at the wallpaper store in our neighborhood, choosing the Victorian reproduction patterns that I believed fit our house. Each room deserved a unique pattern. I chose a plain design for the back stairway and upstairs bathroom and papered them first.

Papering the back stairway was as difficult as doing the front stairway. I used the same equipment and methods as before, but I did not do it in a day. And, as usual, I did the job when Bill was away on the road.

One bedroom was the 10-by-10-foot maid's room at the top of the back stairs. I chose a vibrant pattern to brighten the small room. It was one room that didn't have stained-glass windows. When it was finished, we set up the antique wrought iron bed which baby Bill was born in at home.

There was a large bedroom with an outside front wall and a side wall over the front parlor. Here, I chose a unique Victorian pattern that blended well with the large stained-glass window in each outer wall. This ended up being the favorite room for our frequent guests to "Willie's Hotel."

The Special Gift.

That was the only bedroom big enough to hold our large, three-piece antique bedroom set. The group had a chest of drawers, a vanity stand, a beveled glass mirror, and a matching bed. I had inherited the set from my friend, Maxine, when we lived in Kirksville during the first years of our marriage.

Maxine and her husband were moving to a new apartment over his business. The bedroom set was too big for their bedroom. So, she decided to sell it and buy a smaller set. But it was a family heirloom, passed down to her by her mother. When her mother heard of Maxine's plan to sell it, she protested.

Her mother and I had become good friends. One day, Maxine asked her mother, "What if we give the bedroom set to Bonnie?"

"Yes, you can give it to Bonnie," her mother agreed. "But you can't sell it."

And that's how I ended up with the beautiful bedroom set, which Bill and I used for many years. We have passed it on to our daughter, Susan, who promised to keep passing it down in our family.

The Best for Last.

The other two upstairs bedrooms were across the hall

from each other, above the family and dining rooms. Each bedroom had a wood-burning fireplace and large stained-glass windows on each side of the fireplaces.

I finished the north bedroom with a pretty Victorian patterned wallpaper. We completed the room with some nice pieces of antique bedroom furniture I had collected. This was another favored guest room.

Bill and I chose the south bedroom for ourselves, with its unusual walk-in closet. The other bedrooms didn't have that kind of closet. And he liked it because it was on his side of our bed. I was more flexible.

We chose the paper for our bedroom together. He didn't like "gaudy colors." We compromised and picked a subdued pattern that satisfied us both.

I bought a massive mahogany antique bed at an estate sale for a low price because it was too large for most bedrooms. It had 8-by-8-inch posts beside the ornate, 7-foot headboard and a 3-foot curved footboard. The bed's varnish was dark. It looked like someone had painted it black. You couldn't see the mahogany grain, but I knew when I stripped and refinished the wood, it would be beautiful. And I was never opposed to taking on a worthwhile project.

With two side chairs next to the fireplace, that was plenty of furniture for the room. Many nights, Bill and I enjoyed sitting or reclining in bed, watching the flickering flames in the fireplace.

At last, I had finished the wallpapering. Spring was on the way and the crocus was breaking through the ground and blooming, while other plants began greening up. I could now begin my plans for the outside of our house and the yard.

We'd settled into our life on Park Place. Bill was enjoying his driving job, and I was working full time in nursing. And, when the weather permitted, I continued my flying lessons.

Finally Flying.

Bill had bought our Cessna 150 when we moved to Park Place and kept it in a hangar at a small airport close to Wichita. We'd planned for both of us to learn to fly and get our pilot's licenses.

Bill and our plane

While checking around for my flight instructor, I heard about a young minister who had a good reputation for his students passing their test and getting licensed. Except he had never soloed one of his female students.

When I met him, I was impressed with his pleasant, respectful, and outgoing personality. He would accept me as a student, and I hired him on the spot. Thinking back, I wonder if he thought I would be another woman he would not solo and was just humoring me.

Bill had a heart attack when he was forty-seven—seven years ago—and recovered well. We found out that regulations required him to have a heart catheterization to get a pilot's license. He chose not to do that. I was relieved, because as a nurse, I had seen the procedure cause serious heart problems. In some extreme cases, death.

In reality, he was not as eager as me to become a pilot. He would grin and say, "I can climb as high as anyone as long as I can keep one foot on the ground." Eventually I realized he bought the plane for me, remembering how I had wanted to fly from the time I was a little girl.

I had been excited to start flying lessons, knowing nothing about an airplane except what I could see. My instructor showed me patience through all my many lessons.

Soloing and a Shirttail.

Gradually, I became comfortable with take-offs and landings. We flew to other small airports doing "touch-and-go's," without stopping. I sometimes practiced stopping and taking off again. And I liked practicing climbing high until the plane stalled, then controlling the plane as it dropped and leveled off. My instructor had me doing maneuvers I might experience and teaching me how to regain control. It was all so exciting.

After I had many lessons, my instructor started saying, "When you solo—" and reminding me of previous lessons. One day, as we were landing, he said, "When you solo—"

I cut him off. "Oh, if you only knew how bad I want to solo!"

He looked surprised, maybe panicked. "Really?"

As I landed the plane, he said, "Pull over to the side and stop."

When we were fully stopped, he climbed out of the plane, instructing me non-stop. I looked at him and I swear he was several shades paler than usual.

"Take the plane back on the runway and take it up," he said, a bit uneasily. "Circle around and do a touch-and-go."

My stomach fluttered in anticipation! I got back on the runway, fired up the engine, and took off again... by myself!

I flew back around and touched the runway. My instructor circled his arm in a motion for me to fly up again. After doing a couple more touch-and-go's, he motioned for me to pull over to the side of the runway and stop.

He ran toward me, laughing and shouting, "I could hug you!"

"I'm a hugger!" I hollered back. So, we hugged each other. But it wasn't over yet.

We got back in the plane and rolled over to our hangar and jumped out. He said with a smile, "When you solo for the first time, the custom is to cut off your shirttail and write the date you first soloed on it."

"I have worn this blouse for several weeks to 'sacrifice' the tail when I first soloed," I answered. I had already heard about this and was eager to do it.

He grinned. "We need some scissors."

"I have a pair in my purse." I had a short jacket over my blouse.

I grabbed my purse and quickly dug out the scissors. He

took them and cut the back out of my blouse. The jacket covered the missing part of my shirt.

"We'll have to go to the office to get a pen to write on your shirttail."

I shook my head, smiling. "No! Guess what! I have a magic marker in my purse, too." I had definitely come prepared.

He took the pen I dug out of my purse, and he wrote today's date on my shirttail, and initialed it.

I was so excited that day I first soloed. And it was the first time my instructor soloed a woman. I hope it wasn't his last time.

Disappointment at First.

Eager to get my pilot's license, I studied hard for the written test. My instructor referred me, and I took the test and passed it. He then referred me to a Designated Pilot Examiner (DPE) for my flight test. She worked at an airport on the east side of town. For the flight test, I flew our plane to her airport and landed.

She boarded the plane and had me do a take-off and a landing, also a couple touch-and-go's. Then she had me do a stall, which I did successfully. After that, she instructed me to fly back to her airport, land, pull over, and stop.

I sat there, heart racing in expectation, waiting for the wonderful words I wanted to hear.

She looked straight at me with a serious expression. "You are not ready to get your pilot's license. You need more practice with your instructor." Climbing out of the plane, she walked away without a backward glance.

I was heartbroken. I flew back to the airport where our plane was hangared, then drove home. Bill was away on his job.

Sobbing, I called my flight instructor, telling him how the DPE said I needed more practice.

"Hold on! I know you are ready for your flight test," he protested. "I know another DPE who will do the flight test with you."

He made the arrangements and that DPE met me where our plane was kept. We climbed inside and he told me to roll out to the runway and take off, flying up into the sky. I did so, worried but confident.

He had me doing stalls and other maneuvers to test my ability to control the plane. One maneuver was tipping one wing down and flying around in a circle. He told me he was a stunt pilot, and smiling, suggested I may want to become one: a stunt pilot. I felt much better now.

Another Dream Comes True.

After handling all the maneuvers well, he said, "You are ready for your pilot's license. I'll sign off for you to get it." He directed me to fly back to the airport.

When we landed, my instructor was waiting for us, excited for me.

It only took me forty-five years from the time I first saw an airplane flying in the sky and wanting to fly one myself. After getting my pilot's license, I often took my pre-school grandkids up flying in the morning. They may have thought all grannies took their grandkids in an airplane, just as we sometimes took them for a Sunday drive.

Something Different.

When our kids were still living at home, our family sometimes went on vacation to my brother Murrel's Arabian horse ranch in Colorado. He moved to a large ranch in California as he became internationally known as an Arabian horse breeder and trainer. One year, Bill and I took our extended vacation to drive to the California ranch.

In the summer of 1981, I flew by airline—not in my small plane—to California to visit Murrel. I enjoyed riding the beautiful horses when I wanted. While visiting with him, he told me he wanted to get his Arabians into the Midwest for marketing. He would hold training clinics and classes and show his horses in local and area horse shows. I talked with Bill about the plan. He was surprised, but not too much, and was interested in checking out the matter further.

Our son, Charlie, and his wife, Connie, lived at the Haysville Saddle Club south of Wichita in their new mobile home. They took care of the 2-acre grounds for their rent. When I mentioned Murrel's idea, they were interested in the plan.

Connie had a realtor's license and started looking for a suitable acreage to set up a barn and horse stables. She found a 10-acre plot near Bentley, northwest of Wichita. The property had a mobile home, a hay barn, and several stalls in place. But who would pay for it? Of course, I would, or maybe Bill and I would make the payments for the ranch.

Horses 'R Us.

When I told Murrel about the almost perfect set-up, he was excited and pleased. He agreed to send some of his prize Arabian horses when we were ready for them.

Eager to try this new venture, Charlie and Connie moved their mobile home to our new ranch. As at their last location, they would take care of the horses and clean the stalls to pay for their rent. It would be a monumental task, but they wanted to do it. Their daughter, Tracy, would attend the elementary school close by.

That fall, we told Murrel we were ready for his horses. To our surprise, he sent his driver with a truck and a horse trailer with eight horses. We hadn't expected that many. There were two stallions, two mares-in-foal, and a variety of other horses. A lot of animals to take on at once.

With marketing and selling the Arabians expected, Murrel knew we would need help with caring, training, and showing them. He sent his grown daughter, LeAnn, with them. She had experience with all of that. She came to help the horses, and us, to adjust to the new situation.

After Charlie and Connie felt comfortable feeding and watering the horses and cleaning the stables, LeAnn returned to California. She was engaged, with a wedding date set for the next New Year's Eve.

Soon after getting married, she and her husband, Audy, came to live on our ranch, in the mobile home already there. She worked full time with us, and Audy was employed off the ranch.

LeAnn spent her time working and training the horses,

preparing them to perform in clinics and shows. The bigger task was teaching Charlie, Connie, and especially me how to ride and show the horses.

In less than a year, Audy got a good job offer in Texas. So, he and LeAnn left our ranch. But we had learned a lot from her by then.

Showing Arabians.

Charlie, Connie, and I were each working full time, but we still found time to enter local horse show competitions. We showed and earned ribbons, showing Arabians in a class called "Showmanship at Halter." When doing that, a person on the ground led the horse wearing a halter through a series of maneuvers. The purpose is to display the horse's confirmation and quality of breeding stock.

Connie and I showed horses at the Kansas State Fair in Hutchinson. She showed at-halter and won a third-place ribbon. I showed in the women's western riders' class and won fourth place. I had been nervous about entering, but Bill encouraged me to enter the competition.

Wanting to look good in the competition, I made a black western shirt with decorative silver trim. To complete my outfit, I bought a black western-style hat, jeans, and black boots. I rode a beautiful bay Arabian mare.

Encountering a Womanizer.

Before the competition, I donned my special outfit, mounted the western-style saddle, and waited for the show to begin. An older Arabian horse owner/rancher walked up beside my mare's head and started talking to me. I had never seen him before. He asked my name and who I was riding for. I thought little about the conversation.

Suddenly, Bill walked up and stepped right in front of the stranger. Without speaking to him or saying anything to me, Bill straightened the leg of my jeans and dusted my boot.

His actions confused me, but I couldn't see the other man's face now. I did see him walk away. Bill didn't say anything in explanation, and I didn't ask for one.

Later, I told the story to a friend who knew about the man. She said he was locally known and considered a "womanizer." Maybe so, but he hadn't said anything disrespectful to me. And Bill made sure he never had time to do it.

Horses and Bill.

Bill was on a long layoff from his job but receiving good unemployment benefits from J.I. Case. He now had time to hang out at the stables. He said he wasn't interested in riding horses or being around them. But that changed.

Sometimes we went to the ranch together when I had a day off. I would saddle a horse and ride around in the arena, practicing for riding in a horse show. Bill contented himself with cleaning the stalls.

The horses had a different idea.

Bill was soft-spoken and gentle with them. As he busied himself around the stalls, occasionally a horse would slowly come up behind him to rest their head on his shoulder. He would reach around and pat them. He started using the excuse of combing their mane and brushing them to be close to them. So much for his claim of not liking horses.

Horse Training Clinic.

Murrel and some of his crew came to Wichita to hold a day-long horse training clinic, using the Arabians on our ranch. Then he had a day-long horse show competition, including all breeds of horses and using some local judges. There were also many quarter horses in the clinic and in the competition. The two-day clinic and show were held in a large arena in Wichita.

I made the arrangements and did the pre-planning for the two events. It was a monumental task that started weeks before and lasted a couple of weeks afterward. But it was worth all the effort. Both events made significant money. With all my work, I was too busy to ride in the competition. Charlie and Connie both showed at Halter and won ribbons.

Competing in the American Royal.

In September after the clinic and show, we loaded up our four-horse trailer and headed to Kansas City to attend and enter the competition at the annual American Royal. As a small child, I heard of it, but never dreamed I would compete in it someday.

The American Royal started out as a cattle show, but they later added horse shows. Charlie and Connie entered the at Halter competition, and I entered the women's western riders' competition. Again, I would wear my black western outfit and ride my bay mare.

They both took ribbons with our prize Arabians, and I was proud of them. In my competition, there were dozens of riders. I didn't win anything, but the opportunity and experience were something I will always remember.

Selling the Ranch.

Before long, it seemed everything in our lives started to change. Charlie's company offered him a position with better pay in Oklahoma City. He made the wise decision to move there. They moved their mobile home and took one young Arabian stallion with them.

The "Arabian Experiment" was not proving profitable. We were living in quarter horse country, and Arabians were much higher priced than most breeds. Murrel decided to move and sell the horses to other Arabian owners, mostly further east and south.

I had a nursing career in the making, which I loved. Bill and I had plans for vacations and more time together. Our family was growing, with grandkids and great-grandkids being added often. We sold the ranch and moved on with our lives.

Chapter Six
FOCUS ON NURSING

Helping Other Nurses.

Upon getting my bachelor's degree in nursing from WSU, I joined the Kansas State Nurses Association, District Six. The members presented continuing education classes for nurses and supported nursing students with fundraising for nursing scholarships, among many other activities. I was excited to be a part of this.

It fully occupied me these days working full time, flying my airplane, riding horses, and spending time with Bill and our family. And I had restored our home on Park Place inside and out. Still, I was determined to make time to be part of this worthy organization.

In the summer of 1982, our district six members started making plans to celebrate one hundred years of nursing in Wichita. We wanted a unique way to do this and raise money for scholarships.

Our Victorian house was over one hundred years old, known as the Steinbuschel Home. Since it had been the home of a well-known local doctor, his wife, and family in the early twentieth century, I thought it would be the perfect place to have a unique celebration. When I offered to hold a fundraising tour of our home, the members readily agreed and started planning the tour.

We set a date for the weekend of October 22, 23, and

24, from 9 a.m. to 6 p.m. Tickets could be purchased at the door or by mail: adults for $2 and children for $1. This was a reasonable amount.

On October 5, The Wichita Eagle and Beacon published a story about the history of our house and the tour in their weekly Neighbor's Issue. The cover of the issue had a picture of me sitting in front of the house on the low retaining wall.

The Tour.

The fall weather was beautiful on the first day of the tour. When we opened the front door, hopeful but uncertain, we found a line of adults and children waiting for admission. We were all relieved, and I was more than pleased. Children of all ages attended the tour during the weekend.

They placed District Six members throughout the house to welcome the guests. Most of the members wore uniforms or scrubs, representing our nursing career. I wore the "authentic" Victorian dress I made especially for the occasion. We also had historic nursing paraphernalia on display.

The guests entered through the double cathedral doors into the hallway. They expressed their awe as they first saw the magnificent, multi-colored stained-glass windows in the front parlor and the elaborate stairway. The antique furniture they saw also impressed them, as did the antique walnut pump organ. Many times, the guests—especially the children—sat in the inviting chairs and sofas.

Our 4-by-6-foot 1863 Steinway grand piano, with its massive sold rosewood legs, was another big attraction in the parlor. I had spent hours refinishing the beloved piece from the sad condition it had been in when I purchased it. And I had searched out and found used ivory keys in good condition to replace the damaged and missing ones. So, I felt proud when the piano was admired now. Guests often asked if they could play it, and I allowed them the pleasure. Sometimes our members took a few minutes to play on it as well.

Few of our guests, especially the children, had been inside a Victorian house. Nor had they seen elaborate antique furniture like I had collected over the years. House interiors of this period were known for ornamental and lavish decorative style. There would be patterned wallpaper in floral designs, rich colors, and velvet or sateen brocade coverings on the furniture.

One of our members led a small group of guests up the stairs into the hall. First, they would spend a few minutes in our bedroom admiring the three-piece bedroom set, the colorful stained-glass windows, and the fireplace Bill and I enjoyed so much.

The groups would move on to view the other two bedrooms, with more antique furniture, wood-burning fireplaces, and more stained-glass windows. Occasionally, a guest would linger and take some time to sit in one of the wingback chairs upholstered in wine-colored velvet.

The upstairs bathroom with its large, footed porcelain bathtub and matching fixtures also drew much attention. Next to it, the guests saw the former maid's room, at the head of the back stairway.

Downstairs, they led the visitors into our long family-dining rooms, much used by our family for many gatherings.

Both rooms had red, gold, and blue blended stained-glass windows and wood-burning fireplaces. And with the cool weather, we had a fire lit in the fireplaces during the tours. They could savor the aroma of hickory wood.

Guests also enjoyed seeing the massive dining room furniture that was well used during our family's many shared meals. Next, they led the groups into our beautiful remodeled modern kitchen.

Then they went out the kitchen door onto the side back porch and down the steps to the backyard. There they enjoyed seeing my fall flowers in full bloom and looking spectacular. The gazebo dominating the space was a favorite. Guests, particularly the kids, walked into it and climbed up the stairs to the balcony. I spent some time out there with the guests and explained some of its history.

Bonnie in costume for the tour

Throughout the tour, our members talked about the history of nursing and the benefits of a nursing career. Some of the older kids asked about becoming a nurse. Some of them—both girls and boys—said they had already decided to become a nurse. Overall, our historic tour was a tremendous success. We raised thousands of dollars and many guests gave extra donations. The contributions to scholarships were significant and would be much appreciated by future recipients.

And where was Bill all this time? He wisely visited his uncle in Missouri for the weekend.

My Complex Life.

Still working On-Call in the hospital, I had some control over my schedule in my busy life. I worked when I chose and usually where I chose. This allowed me the opportunity to work in most areas of nursing, except Surgery and Labor Delivery.

Working in the Oncology Unit and Intensive Care Unit especially allowed me to develop my nursing skills. Among those skills, I learned to do physical assessments, start IVs, draw blood for lab work, insert gastric tubes, and do tube feedings.

Some of the intensive care nurses were going to WSU for their master's degree in nursing. They attended classes during the week and wanted to only work on weekends. I could usually work full time, sometimes doing twelve-hour shifts or double shifts when they needed me. Then Bill and I could spend long weekends together, often with our family. But everything was about to change.

Changes and Wrongful Termination.

In 1982, they altered funding for hospitals. They implemented a system called Diagnosis Related Groups (DRGs) funding. It determined a higher level of care was needed to admit a patient to the hospital. As a result, admissions declined. The patient census decreased. There was no longer a need for On-Call Nurses. Because of this change, I transferred to the Oncology Unit and worked part time.

Nurses soon noticed managers coming in, some were from out of state. They started doing different evaluations of nurses, especially those over age fifty. Advanced nurses in good standing were being written up for seemingly unjustifiable, non-nursing issues. They received a poor evaluation for the first time in their nursing careers.

At the same time this was happening, some younger nurses expressed the opinion, "When a nurse reaches the age of fifty, they are too old to practice nursing." I was fifty-one. My belief was—and still is—that a nurse is in their prime as they get older.

One by one, older nurses were being terminated without just cause. We reasoned it was not just because of age, but the long-time nurses were making much higher wages than the younger nurses.

I was one of those unjustifiably let go. When we were terminated, some of us were told, "You will never work again as a nurse."

Being "fired" devastated and humiliated me. I didn't tell our kids for many weeks, and I only told Bill.

To secure our nursing careers, some of us sought legal advice concerning our options. The attorney contacted the Department of Aging concerning Age Bias. As terminated nurses, they did not make us aware of the details of a possible investigation. Then they informed us about the representatives of the Kansas Department of Labor (KDOL) who were there. They were considering and assessing what the nurses believed were wrongful evaluations and terminations.

A short time later, investigators reportedly from the KDOL, began interviewing the terminated nurses and evaluating their individual records. After careful assessment, they deleted the wrongful evaluations.

Not Turning Back Now.

The nurses were reinstated into their previous positions and given their former full benefits, including previous wages. Even though they determined my termination unjustified, I spent several weeks not knowing they had erased it from my record. I knew in my mind that I would continue my nursing career. As is often said, "I hadn't come this far to turn back now."

With my record cleared, they offered me my prior position. I declined the offer and moved on in my career.

I Just Want to be a Nurse.

In my childhood dream, I just wanted to be a nurse and take care of sick people. But nursing is so much more than that.

When I started nursing school, I didn't prefer any particular area of practice. I wanted to "do it all." After three years in my career, I was fortunate to have worked in most areas. It was good experience for future decisions in my career.

The places where I worked often required working with older adults in gerontological nursing. It seemed to be the most complex and challenging area, and the most rewarding.

When I began working full time in the Oncology Unit, I got to know the patient's spouses, children, and other family members. I knew the families were an extension of the patient. We included them in the Nursing Plan of Care for the patient.

An important factor in caring for the patients and their family members was preparing for End-of-Life issues and care. We planned and provided the highest level of comfort possible. The plan included implementing and providing intervention and support in the grieving process.

They involved ministers and counselors for the patient and their family in choices of extended care and End-of-Life issues. When appropriate, they dismissed a patient to their home. There they received nursing support as needed, knowing they would probably return to our care for End-of-Life support.

After my wrongful termination and reinstatement, I took many weeks to recover from the traumatic incident. The bright side of the time off was having more time with Bill and our growing family. It gave me additional time to spend on weekends with everyone, picnicking, boating, and waterskiing. And Bill and I took some vacation time, going on historic trips and other fun trips throughout the country.

Nursing Home Charge Nurse.

It was time to start job hunting again. I found ads in the newspaper for nursing positions. Most of them required working every other weekend, but I searched for alternatives.

A nurse friend told me about a good-paying evening Charge Nurse position in a large, well-known nursing home. I called the Director of Nursing (DON) and gave her my name. Then I made an appointment to fill out an application and for an interview with her.

After I arrived there and completed the form, we sat down for the interview. She didn't even look at the application. "You have the position if you want it," the DON said.

I was surprised and pleased. She said she had spoken with several of my former nursing co-workers. Each of them had recommended me for this position. While I appreciated that, I was unsure of what the responsibilities were. I explained I had not worked in a nursing home.

She assured me I would have a thorough orientation. With that assurance, I took the position.

I worked second shift, Monday through Friday. The Friday shift cut into my long weekends with Bill, but he encouraged me to take the position if I wanted it. I could always count on his support.

Respecting Patients.

I understood nursing home care required a different approach from hospital nursing. It is the home of the residents. They are not patients. The resident's room is their home and we respected it as such. We knocked on their door before entering.

There are many levels of care. Some residents are up and about, usually with help from canes or walkers or in wheelchairs. Others were bedfast and required total care. Some were totally alert, while others had varying stages of dementia and other behavioral concerns. I was up for this new challenge.

The primary concern I felt needed immediate attention was how we dealt with a resident's incontinence. Most of them were incontinent to some degree. Though it may sound crude to speak about it, incontinence was a dominant and pressing issue. We were still using washable cloth diapers.

When the Certified Nurse Assistant (CNA) changed a resident's diaper, they had to rinse it out, wring it out with gloved hands, and place it in a closed container. The laundry washed the diapers only on the night shift. There was a high risk of spreading bacteria, not to mention dealing with the odor of the urine and feces.

I felt this situation significantly affected my second shift CNAs, who put clean diapers on residents at bedtime. Sometimes the supply of diapers was low. The CNAs had to make tough decisions about whom to change until laundry could provide clean diapers. Third shift CNAs had to wake the resident to change them.

Suggesting a Change.

During my orientation, I realized this critical problem concerning diapers. I discussed the issue with the DON, and we consulted with our administrator. Disposable diapers were available, but expensive. Cloth diapers were not cheap, either. The time the CNAs spent washing them was also extensive. Laundry staff labor was time-consuming and costly. This was a bad situation.

It pleased me when the administrator agreed to change to disposable diapers and briefs. This gave the CNAs more time to provide personalized skin care for the residents. Not to mention being free from the unpleasant chore and odor of rinsing the cloth diapers.

The change was a major benefit for both residents and CNAs. Another benefit of disposable diapers was their moisture barrier lining, providing some skin protection for the resident. An essential in preventing skin breakdown.

No Problem Helping.

In my position as Charge Nurse, I had the responsibility of making the monthly schedule for the second shift staff. When I first talked with some of them, they told me they would not work with particular residents and only on specific halls. While I respected their opinions, I assured each of them that if they wanted me to schedule them, they would work where I assigned them.

The DON and administrator supported me on the matter. As a result of this, two CNAs resigned, but the administration soon replaced them with other experienced ones. Word got around that our home was a good place to work.

I realized the CNAs were the foundation of resident

care. They provided round the clock personal care. We began including them in our starting shift report each day to be aware of each resident's needs.

I often spent time charting at the front desk. The room lights lit up over the resident's room and at the desk. During my orientation, I sometimes heard the former Charge Nurse respond. She would stand up and shout out for a CNA to answer the light.

If I saw a light come on, though, and I knew the CNAs were busy elsewhere, I went to the resident's room. I had no problem helping with a resident's needs. When the CNA came to respond to the light, it surprised them to find me there. But if they needed help, I again offered to do it. Before they got to know me, they would say, "Oh, no. I'll get someone else to help me."

I'd say, "Do you not think I can do it?" With the situation eased, we would laugh and do what needed to be done for the resident.

At mealtime, I went to the dining room with the staff. I helped serve trays and visited with the residents. Some of the CNAs had to feed bedfast residents in their rooms. Some residents in the dining room required assistance, and I helped with them as needed. It was a good way to become acquainted with the residents.

Appreciation.

After a short time, the residents' families told me—and the DON and the administrator—how pleased they were with the improved care on second shift. The administrator was getting phone calls from family members. He would bring me a note about a call he'd received and hand it to me, smiling.

I continued working in the nursing home through the winter months. It was a pleasant place to work. The licensed staff and the CNAs developed a good relationship with each other, the residents, and families. The DON and administrator were pleased and appreciated my efforts. At ninety days, they gave me a superior evaluation and a substantial pay increase.

How could I want a better place to practice my profession and continue to develop my nursing skills and apply my body of knowledge?

Age Never Defined Me.

Two years after graduation, I renewed my Bachelor of Science in Nursing (BSN) license as required through continuing education classes for nurses. Soon it would be time to renew my license for another two years. Time was passing quickly.

I often thought about talking with the RNs at the hospital where I'd worked, about how they were pursuing their Master of Science in Nursing (MSN) degree. They had told me about the advanced nursing classes in the behavioral sciences, statistics, and research. I was fifty-four, not that age ever defined who I was or what I wanted to do. And I felt a desire to increase my nursing knowledge.

I found out WSU had a position for MSN students to work as a Graduate Teaching Assistant (GTA) while working on their master's degree. This would be a challenge since the

MSN and the GTA positions were both full-time. But when had a challenge ever stopped me before?

I wasn't sure how Bill would feel about my thoughts, my plans. The conversation we'd had when I first told him I wanted to go to nursing school in my thirties ran through my mind. "You've worked hard all your life! Why don't you just take it easy now?" he'd said.

Yet I couldn't let this idea drop without talking to him about it. Nervous but determined, I brought the subject up with him one day. Then held my breath to wait for his response. .

My ever-supportive husband looked at me, smiled. "Go for it!"

I released my breath and grinned back at him, eager to get started with the next part of my career.

Moving Past a Dream.

Before classes started, Bill and I sold our Cessna 150 airplane. He had recovered from his heart attack. But he'd refused getting the heart catheterization required by law for him to get a pilot's license. He wasn't as "airworthy" as I was. He didn't enjoy flying in a small plane like I did. Owning our plane had saved us more than the price we paid for it because we would have had to rent a plane for my flying lessons.

That one childhood dream had come true: I'd flown an airplane. I'd gone a big step past that in owning a plane. It was time to move past that dream. I'd accomplished it and I'd had the opportunity to take our grandkids flying with me. Something we would all remember.

Decision made, we sold our plane for more than we paid for it.

Never Understood the Word Quit.

Spring of 1985, I began this next career step. I took and passed the college entrance exam for admission into WSU's master's program in nursing. I would start classes that fall. Because of this new plan, I gave notice to the DON and administrator of the nursing home where I was working. They were gracious enough to thank me for having worked there and wished me well.

In my new GTA position, I assisted the nursing faculty with teaching Bachelor of Nursing Students. I taught in the classroom, administered tests, and graded papers. And I worked with the students in the hospitals for their clinical experience and practicum, which meant the faculty didn't need to do it. They credited most of my GTA hours toward my MSN degree.

A research class was one of my first classes in the MSN program. There were about a hundred of us in the class. The lectures provided unfamiliar information of importance to us. As always, I enjoyed learning something new that would help me in my career. They required us to do papers that required statistics and behavioral sciences input. This was a traumatic and stressful start toward the advanced degree.

About half of the students made a D or an F at the end of the class, proving how hard it had been. I made a D, not a passing grade in nursing. We couldn't continue with the failing grade but could retake the class or drop out of the program. Nearly half of those failing-grade students left the program. I refused to give up and retook the class. I'd never in my life understood the word "quit."

I also didn't want to give up working with my nursing students as a GTA. We had developed professional friendships and relationships that I enjoyed. I thrived in the role of teaching and realized the benefits and joys of doing so, and of the impact it had on my students.

With my decision made not to quit, I prepared to retake the research class. Some of the nursing faculty at WSU had their Doctorate in Nursing, and I took my class with one of them. The first day of class was a positive experience, and I felt confident about passing this time.

That Age Issue Again.

After that first week of classes, I believed I had chosen the right professor. One day, as I walked out, she stood by the classroom door. She motioned me away from the other students, and quietly asked, "Bonnie, what are you doing here? You're not going to live long enough for this to help you."

I was stunned. I didn't see being fifty-four as a problem. Maybe it was more than just my age that worried her, though she didn't mention it.

Before starting the master's program, I let my tinted hair go to its natural color: silver white. I inherited the white hair from Daddy and his father. I had colored my hair for over twenty years before it started turning gray in my thirties. Stopping coloring my hair made my hair easier to care for while in school. And Bill liked the silver-white color.

There was nothing wrong with this. As with "age," my appearance should not define me! I would prove her wrong.

By the end of the semester, I aced the research class.

1985 Bonnie

Going on with Life.

As demanding as nursing school was, I still put Bill and our family first. Being a wife and mother were most important to me. We continued with family get-togethers whenever we could manage them.

Charlie and his family were now living in Oklahoma. John was driving over the road. The grandkids were growing, and more were coming along.

Bill and I attended church services when we could. We continued our offering, but didn't often attend other church activities, except for Christmas, Easter, and other holiday festivities.

Most of the time, I could complete my schoolwork during the week while Bill was driving for work. When I needed to study on the weekend, he cooked or took us out to eat. Eating out wasn't his preference since he had to do that on his job. He preferred my cooking, but, as always, he did what was most helpful for me.

I didn't have nursing students in the summer semester and took two master's degree classes instead. Bill and I took vacations the two weeks before and the two weeks after the summer classes. We took extended trips to historic sites like the Alamo, Gettysburg Battlefield, and New Orleans, among other places.

After our usual holiday times with our family, Bill and I spent time with our families in Missouri. We also enjoyed going to Branson, Missouri at Christmas time. The parades and non-stop Christmas music were a big draw for us. The time away from nursing school and students was fun and relaxing.

As I got close to finishing my MSN degree, I felt encouraged. With my efforts, help, and support from others, I stayed on the Honor Roll and got all "A's" in my classes. I couldn't have been prouder.

Chapter Seven
LIFE COMPLICATIONS

Proving Myself.

The doctoral professor of nursing who had questioned me earlier about what I was doing in school now at my age and I developed a close relationship. Neither of us mentioned the issue again. I knew what I wanted to do with my career and why. And I proved to her that age didn't matter.

In my next-to-last semester, I needed to take another class that she taught. Assuming that went well from here on out, I would graduate in May after the spring semester.

"I'll call an ambulance!"

Bill had not been to his cardiologist for over a year. Even though it was difficult to schedule an appointment, I encouraged—okay, nagged—him to go to the doctor. As stubborn as me, he kept putting off meeting with someone.

He usually got home from one of his road trips in the night when I was asleep.

The weekend before Thanksgiving, on a night just before dawn, I woke up as he came into our bedroom.

He sat down on the side of the bed without turning on a light. "I guess I had better get to that doctor," he said in his quiet voice.

"Good. I'll make an appointment in the morning," I said, half asleep yet alert, too.

When he didn't respond, I sat up, alarmed. "Do you mean you need to see the doctor now? Right now?"

"Yes."

Heart racing, I hollered, "I'll call an ambulance!"

He shook his head. "No, no. I have to shave first." He turned on the lights and went to shave at the sink. That stubborn streak making it clear I would not persuade him otherwise.

Ignoring his attitude, I jumped up and got dressed as fast as possible. "I'm calling an ambulance right now!"

Again, he gave me an obstinate look. "No. You can drive me to the emergency room."

I could see he was pale and shaky, but I would not change his mind. Thankfully, the hospital was only a few blocks away from where we lived.

When we got to the hospital emergency room (ER), the staff lifted Bill into a wheelchair. They rushed him to the Intensive Care Unit, where they admitted him to the hospital.

I had the following week off from classes, though I could have missed some if necessary to spend time with Bill. Which, of course, I would have done.

We didn't have our usual family Thanksgiving dinner the Sunday before the holiday. Instead, our kids spent as much time as possible with Bill and me at the hospital.

The doctors determined he needed a triple bypass surgery to correct his massive heart attack within two days. They scheduled it for soon after Thanksgiving, with Bill remaining in the hospital until then. During all of this, our church and other friends offered many much-appreciated prayers.

When classes resumed after Thanksgiving, I told the nursing faculty and my doctoral professor about Bill's heart attack. They were supportive, expressed their concern, and did all they could to lessen my workload. I still had to finish tests and papers before the end of the semester to prevent getting incomplete grades.

Priorities and Concerns.

While all of that mattered to me, Bill was my top priority and concern. I knew his condition and surgery could be life-threatening. In his typical upbeat manner, he encouraged me to complete my work for the semester. He understood that if I got even one incomplete in class, I could not finish my degree in the spring and graduate. That was unacceptable to both of us, since I had worked so hard for this.

His surgery went well, thank the good Lord. With follow-up rehab, he began his recovery. As usual, he was positive. They discharged him from the hospital in a couple of weeks, giving him strict follow-up orders. Even with all this, he insisted I finish my classwork for the semester.

I struggled with my tests and papers, but I completed them all, except one. It was an in-depth paper for my doctoral professor's class. I accepted the sad fact that I couldn't get it done on time, and it weighed on me. When I told the professor, she said, "Go ahead and finish the paper and give it to me as soon as you can."

When I told Bill what the professor told me, his stubborn streak came out again. He insisted I take the time to complete the paper. With his support and my determination, I finished it and turned it in just a couple of days after the deadline.

It took several days to receive our grades for the semester. The professor mailed me a copy of my paper, giving me an "A" on it. I made an "A" in her class and in all the others.

Bill was recovering. With all our family, we made plans for the Christmas holidays. My prayers were being answered, but there would be a challenging time ahead of us. I hoped, planned, and prayed to graduate in the spring. It depended on whether Bill continued his recovery if I could handle the last semester of classes.

Staying Positive.

My last semester would begin in the middle of January 1988. After Christmas, I took Bill to rehab Monday through Friday. Recovering well, they gave him permission to walk up and down the many stairways in our home. The doctor also allowed him to drive by the time I started the spring classes. But he could not drive over the road in his job.

Because he was a Teamsters Union member, Bill had wonderful health insurance with J.I. Case. It covered all his hospital, doctor, and rehab expenses. A great relief to us. He continued receiving full health and disability insurances. He was sixty-two when he had his heart surgery. Both insurances lasted until he was sixty-eight.

His disability coverage was about three-fourths of what he would have made working forty hours a week. It allowed us not to worry about having income while I finished my MSN degree.

The semester began with a full load of classes. Bill was

up and around, doing a lot of the cooking and housework. I remained aware there was the chance he might not fully recover, or he could have a setback and be partially disabled... or worse. We tried to stay positive and encouraged each other.

By March, Bill felt he had recovered enough to take a road trip on his own. He drove to Missouri to visit his bachelor uncle Carl in the family home place of his grandparents. Then he drove to Jefferson City and visited his two sisters who lived in and near the city. After being gone for two weeks, he returned refreshed. I had encouraged him to go but prayed for his safety and for his return home.

Bill's New Dream.

Now that he had retired, Bill wanted to move to the country after I graduated in the spring. It meant selling our house at Park Place that I had worked so hard on and loved. But I knew it was just "a place." We would take our "home" with us wherever we went.

Throughout our marriage, he had always helped me have what I wanted and much more. It seemed he made all my childhood dreams come true, and more that I didn't know to dream of as a child. This was my turn. I encouraged him to do and have what would make him happy at this time in our life.

After contacting a realtor we knew, we started looking at houses in the country on small acreages. We listed our house, knowing few people wanted a registered landmark house and the responsibilities that go with it. Few could afford the price, either.

Then our realtor told us about a couple in California moving back to Wichita and who were interested in our house. The wife had accepted a management position at the airport. Her husband was finishing his Doctorate in Ministry and had been hired in a position in Wichita. They were moving to town at the end of his spring semester.

The couple had seen pictures of our house and talked with realtors about its history and condition. They wanted it enough to sign a contract without seeing it in person. They would close on the house after they moved to Wichita, and they had up-front cash to pay for our beautiful Victorian home.

Final Hectic Semester.

The last few weeks of the semester were hectic, but Bill, as always, was there for me. He enjoyed his retirement and made it possible for me to devote full time to my classes and student teaching.

We didn't have to do a thesis as an MSN student if we weren't planning to go on for a Doctoral Degree in Nursing, which I wasn't. I took extra classes in Nursing Administration and did projects related to nursing practice.

One project, which many of us chose, was an extemporaneous written dialog on a nursing practice issue. The paper involved applying the behavioral sciences, pharmacology, and other nursing practice issues, along with patient care.

One Saturday morning, we went into a large classroom and sat in desks spaced a distance apart. They provided us with a pencil and sheets of blank paper. Three professors monitored us and would later read and grade our papers. The professors would not know who authored a paper until after the grading process.

They gave us a nursing subject to write on and assigned each of us a code. We started writing promptly at ten o'clock, and they stopped us at twelve o'clock. The papers were several pages long.

It took two weeks before the papers were all graded. Each professor assigned a pass or fail grade to each paper the first time they read it. If the paper received two passing grades, they approved the paper. I heard they sometimes read the papers more than once before they decided a final grade. My graduation depended on passing the critical project.

Words That Meant a Lot.

After identifying my name with my paper, one professor came to me with my graded paper. She smiled as she handed it to me. "Your paper was one of only four papers which each of the professors gave a passing grade on the first reading."

Her words meant a lot to me and made me confident that I would graduate. With that in mind, I had one-hundred graduation announcement cards printed. I mailed them to siblings, other family members, and friends. I did not mean them specifically as invitations. I was just in a happy, bragging mood, which Bill noticed.

Since we had a contract for the sale of our house, it pressed us to look for our "new home" in the country.

New Lake Waltanna Home.

Our realtor told us about a housing development around a manmade lake called Lake Waltanna. The odd name came from the developer and his wife: Walt and Anna. Most of the houses were owned by professionals: doctors, lawyers, and business owners.

As we drove into the area, the elegant brick homes struck us. Most of them were on two-acre lots. They all had natural wood shingles, as composite roofs were not allowed.

I asked the realtor, "What are we doing here?" I knew we didn't have that kind of money to spend on a home such as these.

He said there is one house that might work for us. The house was in bankruptcy and had been vacant for many months. The owner wanted to sell the house for whatever he could get.

We drove into the driveway of a beautiful brick, two-story house with a two-car garage and a short, covered walk to the front door. A slight hillside at the back of the house took us to the enclosed swimming pool area. The large pool's water had thick blue-green algae, and we couldn't see the color of the pool tile.

The realtor told us the asking sale price was about half of what it would be if the house had been in good condition. Bill and I had done restoration before, but never to this extent. But we decided to see the entire house before deciding.

Double sliding glass doors led into the dinette area, suitable for a small dinette set. The kitchen had a sizeable window over the sink that overlooked the lake. Wooden cabinets were beautiful and in excellent condition. And the appliances, including an electric glass-top stove, matched.

Next, we came to a family room, about four feet below ground level, with wood-paneled wainscotting on the walls. A wide sliding glass window allowed in plenty of light and breezes when desired. On one side of the room was a massive brick wood-burning fireplace with a large mirror over it. I could imagine a sofa, recliners, and a TV arranged to enjoy a flickering fire in the fireplace.

Heading down the hallway, we passed a closet housing the central heat and air conditioner units, which we hadn't had before. And we learned the house had a built-in vacuum cleaner system, something I had never heard of but thought would be nice.

A divided staircase led up to the front door's landing. We noted decorative handrails were in place of an upstairs inside wall above the stairway.

The lower level had two bedrooms and a full bath with two sinks. One bedroom had a large closet and large sliding glass windows on the side wall. The other bedroom was the master, with two closets I thought would be good to have. I also liked the double sliding glass doors that opened onto the walk by the pool area.

On the upper level were a large family room and a dining room with a wood-burning fireplace. Large, double sliding glass doors opened onto a walkout balcony with ornate metal handrails on each end of the room.

This level also had another full bathroom and two more bedrooms. The bedrooms had sizeable sliding glass doors with walkout balconies that overlooked the pool. They had a beautiful view of the lake and colorful landscaping.

Overall, the house appealed to Bill and me, even though there would be much to do to it. All the carpeting needed to be professionally cleaned or replaced before we moved in. I could paper and paint the walls to my taste.

The realtor explained that even after paying the realtor's fee, we would get enough for the sale of our house on Park Place to pay for this house. Even with all the restoration needed here, we felt "at home." We signed the contract for the house that day. We had no way of knowing that the Lake Waltanna house would be our home for fifteen years.

Letting Go of the Steinway.

The couple buying our Park Place house surprised us. They closed and paid full price for it three weeks before my graduation. We then bought our new home at Lake Waltanna. But we found we were about $2,000 short of what we needed. As always, Bill figured the problem out.

There was so much we needed to do, including my college issues. I completed the remaining work with my students and took tests and finished papers for the semester.

At the same time, my friends who did estate sales came in and helped us prepare for a one-day sale. We didn't have room for many of our antiques in the country home. There was the Victorian sofa, the ornate walnut reed pump organ, and our massive Victorian mahogany bed. We had enough Victorian side tables and chairs to hold a sale.

We also didn't have room for the museum-quality Steinway grand piano. One of the sale's customers had heard about the piano and came to see it. She contacted her brother, a doctoral professor, and head of the music department at a Texas college. He paid our asking price of $4,500 and had it shipped to his college. I had paid $200 for it but spent over a thousand dollars having it restrung after I refinished it. We were sad to see it go, but we had many years of memories with it.

Waiting for Me to Finish.

Bill's health and well-being were always on my mind, but he was a take-charge person. He soon had the carpet cleaned at our new home. After the sale, he, our family, and friends started moving small furniture and packed boxes. Kathi was great help boxing kitchen items and stocking our new kitchen.

Their efforts let me focus on completing what I needed to do for school. Bill hired a moving van to haul the last of our furniture the day we gave over possession of our home by midnight. Except I was still working on my final paper. We left a small chair and table, where I had my computer and printer in the maid's room. At 8 p.m., I printed out my paper. Bill was waiting somewhere.

I called out his name.

Smiling, he walked upstairs to my room. He told me he had been sitting on the steps waiting for me to finish.

I carried the computer and printer downstairs and out to our pickup. Bill brought the table and chair. One last time, Bill locked the door, and we headed to our new home in the country.

Special Honor.

Soon I would have my Master's Graduation Ceremony and walk across the stage. The bachelor's degree students had their usual Pinning Ceremony and received their much-valued nursing pin.

They asked me to be one of the speakers at their ceremony. It was an honor that had not been given to a Graduate Teaching Assistant before.

A Little Bragging.

The grades were all in and I made it! Graduation day, May 21, 1988, was coming soon. Even though I mailed dozens of announcements to family and friends, I had not heard from many of them.

They were announcements—not invitations, so I could brag just a little bit. I rationalized that not much interest was just like my siblings. But I expected some congratulation cards for their "Big Sister, Little Sister."

Our grown kids all had busy lives. John was driving over the road for work. Charles and his family now lived in Oklahoma. Kathi was working in a management position out of town. Susan and her family attended my graduation. But we were all together the previous Sunday for Mother's Day.

Something Is Going On.

I suspected that something was happening. Unknown to me, Bill had made plans. He had intercepted the phone calls and mail while I was busy finishing classes. He and my family were planning a surprise Graduation Party for me.

Early Saturday morning, Bill and I were heading to the WSU campus for the graduation ceremony. He said we would meet with some of the family and friends there and attend the ceremony together.

When we got to their agreed upon meeting place, over twenty of my family and friends were waiting for me. Some of my siblings came from California, Colorado, Texas, and other states. Several others lived in Wichita, where those from out of town had stayed.

I was so surprised and definitely pleased. We greeted each other with hugs and smiles. Then we filed into the auditorium where they held the ceremony. Bill and the others sat together in good view of the stage.

My Proud Moment.

With my cap and gown in hand, I walked down front and joined the other graduates. We donned our caps and gowns and sat in front of the stage. Excitement thrummed through me. I had worked so long and hard for this moment.

After a long speech by the WSU official, he called each graduate's name for them to walk across the stage. When he called mine, I was so proud of my accomplishments. He handed me my graduate degree. I accepted it and continued walking, head high and smiling.

WICHITA STATE UNIVERSITY
Commencement
May 21, 1988

1988 Bonnie graduating

When the ceremony was finished, I joined Bill, my family, and friends. We all walked out together to our cars.

Since it was near lunchtime, I asked Bill, "Should we all go to a restaurant together?"

"I have it all taken care of," he said.

Memorable Occasion.

It was over twenty miles to our home in the country. I wondered what he had meant but didn't ask. As we drove away from the campus, the others pulled out behind us and followed us home. Some of them had been to our new home already.

While we were parking and visiting before going inside, a food van pulled up to our back door. The driver and staff carried food into our dinette room, setting it on the table and kitchen counters. So much food! There were hot, roasted wieners and ham with rolls, bread, casseroles, salads, and desserts. And there were enough drinks for the afternoon.

Thinking back, I remember noticing Bill was spending a lot of time getting rid of the blue-green algae in the swimming pool, preparing it for safe use. He had told our guests about it. Most of them brought their bathing suits and spent a lot of time enjoying it that day.

The man I had loved for so many years had done something special for me yet again. Bill made sure my master's graduation was a memorable occasion. I had the chance to enjoy being with my visiting family for several days before they had to leave.

I will always treasure that wonderful day... and Bill.

Finally Relaxing.

After the graduation party and the guests went home, Bill and I had the pleasure of being alone for the first time in our lives.

His health was good, and he was retired now. I was not yet working outside the home. We enjoyed the freedom of doing tasks—or not—as we chose. We took turns cooking or cooked together, grocery shopped together in Goddard, and occasionally ate out at a nice restaurant in town.

His doctor approved and encouraged him to take two-mile walks around the lake, most mornings before breakfast. Sometimes I walked with him. It seemed I could relax to a greater extent than I had for decades.

Bill liked mowing our two-acre lot with his first-time riding lawnmower. He kept the pool clean and clear. He fished from the shore and from his small motorboat. And he spent a lot of time servicing our car and pickup. He always had a vehicle ready if we decided to take a trip.

With my free time now, I bought wallpaper for the six rooms I wanted to paper. The rooms were painted. I wanted to add my touch. And I enjoyed selecting drapery fabric and making decorative draperies for the many large windows.

We weren't alone. Our family often visited on weekends. They swam in the pool and fished on the shore or in the boat with Bill. Usually, he didn't like to linger if he didn't catch a fish in ten minutes or so, but he did for the grandkids.

Picnic and Reunion.

In the middle of July, we took our usual annual trip to the El Dorado Springs Picnic held on Thursday, Friday, and Saturday. We attended on Saturday. They had held the picnic every year for over a hundred years, with thousands attending. It gave us the chance to visit with former neighbors and old friends while feasting at food booths and listening to nonstop entertainment.

The next day, we went to my Green Ridge School Reunion in a small community outside of town. The one-room school closed in 1942, but we started having reunions after WWII. A local women's group served a huge country buffet. We enjoyed the opportunity to feast, visit, and take pictures with our former classmates all afternoon.

While we were travelling around, Bill decided to visit his siblings and their families around Jefferson City for a couple of days. And we went on to Springfield to see my siblings and their families. After another couple of days, we were ready to head home. It had been a busy but pleasant and relaxing trip.

On returning home, it was a real joy to continue doing what I wanted to do when I wanted to do it. Or not do anything. We worked together as we wanted or did our own thing.

Chapter Eight
LIFE GOES ON

Warm Feeling at Church.

Bill and I were grocery shopping when we passed a small church of our denomination on our way home. It was on a large lot at the edge of Goddard.

The church seemed to call to me. I said to him, "The only thing that would make my life complete is for us to go to church together."

He said nothing, in his usual way of taking time to think things over.

The following Saturday evening, he asked me, "Would you like to go to church in the morning?"

"Sure," I answered in pleasure.

As we arrived at church, friendly people greeted us. There were about fifty adults and children, a small congregation. The pianist played while the choir sang, and the director led the congregation to sing our favorite old gospel hymns.

The young preacher's sermon was one of faith and encouragement, which Bill and I appreciated. After the final hymn and prayer, there was much handshaking and invitations to come back. We left the church with a warm feeling and discussed the experience over dinner at our favorite restaurant. We agreed to attend the church again.

A Lawn Mowin' Fool.

After attending the church a few Sundays, we became members. When we didn't have family and friends at our place fishing and swimming, we began going to the church's evening services.

It didn't take Bill long to notice the two-acre church grounds often needed mowing. He offered to take on the job, bringing his riding mower from home. It gave him pleasure to mow there once or twice a week as needed. When questioned why he volunteered to do it, he said, "I don't teach, and I don't preach. But I'm a lawn mowin' fool." Over many years, he mowed the lawn and saved them thousands of dollars.

We became active in the small church, enjoying our fellow members. Bill took part in the maintenance and finance committees, and I worked with youth groups, and taught adult and children's Sunday school classes.

Bill's Recipes.

Our church had a potluck dinner every month, another great fellowship time, which we enjoyed. Bill often prepared his favorite casseroles and desserts for the dinners. His cooking soon became some of the congregation's favorites.

The church women published a cookbook, sharing everyone's favorite recipes. They asked Bill to include his recipes, and he shared several of them. I was proud of him.

"Get a job."

One evening in late summer, Bill and I had settled into our recliners, eating supper from trays while watching TV. When a commercial came on, he muted the TV and quietly said, "I've been thinking. I think you know, if we were going to stay here, you're gonna have to go to work."

I glanced at him and noted he had a whimsical, but serious, look in his eyes. He was really saying, "Get a job!"

We had both needed this wonderful, relaxing summer, but he was right. I started following up on some job leads from fellow nurse friends and ads in the paper. Soon I had tips on several good possibilities.

I Could Make a Difference.

I found multiple opportunities in my preferred practice in long-term care. One of the nursing homes I considered was advertising for an Assistant DON (ADON). I went for an interview with the DON. She was quite young.

She shared with me that this was her first DON position, and she had interviewed others for the job I was seeking. She told me she knew of my success in staffing in my former job as a DON. Her greatest concern at this facility was keeping staff in place, especially Certified Nurse Assistants (CNAs).

She explained that there were agencies in town who provided health care staff on a contract basis. They were sometimes called "Rent a Nurse." It was a common practice for nursing homes to use agency CNAs. The need for better staffing led to using the agencies.

The DON said she spent much of her time calling agencies to provide adequate staffing for this home to meet state requirements. One problem she ran into was that agency CNAs were paid much more than her CNAs.

The owner of the facility was based in Texas. At her recommendation, the company hired a full-time RN to conduct CNA classes at no charge to the students. When they started classes, they had to sign an agreement to work for the facility for at least ninety days after certification. The RN had been conducting the classes for several months.

Another problem her facility had was even though the CNA students signed a contract to work for them, they couldn't enforce it. After getting certified, most of the students left to work in other facilities where the working conditions and pay were better.

The DON asked if I was interested in the ADON position because of my prior experience. She needed someone to take over some of her responsibilities so she could spend more time doing agency staffing. She worked overtime and was not getting paid extra for it.

With my experience doing staffing and believing I could make a difference, I accepted the position.

Job Challenges.

The DON asked me to make the monthly schedule, which I liked to do. Her current CNA schedule was for four days on, then two days off. When I talked with the CNAs, they didn't like this schedule. They only had a Saturday-Sunday weekend off every six weeks. They said this schedule, along with the low pay, was the main reason for the poor retention of CNAs here.

I had learned that scheduling every other weekend off worked best. When I told the DON about making this change, she didn't think it would work, but I could try it. Retention improved the first month.

Two officials from the Texas corporate office visited us, concerned about why this nursing home was not making money. Most of all, they worried about passing the annual State nursing home survey, which would happen soon. If residents were not receiving standard care, the home risked heavy fines or closure.

To my relief, it pleased the officials to hear about the improvement in staff retention, and they asked if I had any other suggestions. I admitted the cost of the RN and the CNA classes was not a good investment. There were other classes in the city to provide an adequate supply of CNAs. I explained that if we discontinued the classes here, we could increase our CNA pay and not use the agency.

Word soon spread around town that our home was a good place to work. Our CNAs liked being there long enough to get to know the residents. And the residents and their families enjoyed seeing familiar faces and learning the CNAs' names, which improved the quality of life for the residents.

It took a few weeks for our home to no longer need agency staffing. I could increase CNA pay and hire them as needed. The company discontinued the classes, but instead of terminating the RN, she was allowed to "resign" (better for her).

Duly Inducted Honor.

One afternoon when I came home from work, Bill handed me a padded letter-size manilla envelope that arrived in the mail. Curious, I opened it and found an ornate, beautifully printed certificate.

SIGMA THETA TAU

International Society of Nursing
This certifies that
BONNIE LACEY KRENNING
was duly inducted into Sigma Theta Tau
as a member of
EPSILAM GAMMA
WICHITA STATE UNIVERSITY
WICHITA, KANSAS
May 7, 1989

It surprised and amazed me. I had never heard of the organization.

With the help of my daughter, Susan, we investigated the society. It began in 1952 as an international society of nurses. There are now 135,000 members and over five hundred chapters. They induct qualifying nurses into the society based on their excellence in nursing scholarship and community service. The words "SIGMA THETA TAU," translated into English are "LOVE, COURAGE, and HONOR."

Their Mission Statement is: Developing nurse leaders anywhere to improve healthcare everywhere. The society's

Vision is: Create a global community of nurses who lead in knowledge, scholarship, and professional development of nurses to improve the health of people worldwide.

It was an honor to be inducted into the organization as a member of Epsilam Gamma. I would remain a lifelong Sigma Theta Tau member.

"You did it for me."

Even though I was salaried, I often worked overtime without extra pay. While I worked, Bill kept everything going at home. He cooked, shopped for groceries, did the laundry, and cleaning. I drove a half-hour to work, and he made sure my car was in good condition, including keeping it gassed up for me. I appreciated him doing all of this so I could focus on my new job.

One fall evening, I came home from a hard day at work to find Bill had a fire burning and supper ready to set on the table. I smiled, loving this wonderful man so much. "I don't know of another man who would do this."

He looked at me and in his quiet way said, "Well, you did it for me, didn't you?" Few men think that way.

Although he was not mowing lawns now, he walked the two miles around the lake most mornings. It pleased me he kept up with his health needs.

Besides taking care of many household chores, he understood how much I enjoyed our times using the fireplace. One day, Bill installed a fireplace insert that had a temperature control. It allowed him to heat our home with the fireplace when he wanted. And he enjoyed cutting stacks of wood so we could keep the fireplace burning throughout the night.

Anticipating the Holidays.

With my nursing practice going well, I started thinking about and planning for the winter holidays. I also had to consider the staffing at work for Thanksgiving Day and Christmas Day.

Over the decades of our marriage, our family had developed many Thanksgiving traditions, including having our dinner the weekend before the actual holiday. As the day grew closer, we were all excited about our first holiday dinner at Lake Waltanna. Charlie, Connie, and their teenage daughter were coming from Oklahoma City for the weekend. Our other families, including five more grandkids, lived close by and would be there for the dinner.

With Bill retired and feeling well, he enjoyed planning and shopping for our big meal. He asked me if I had anything to add to his grocery list, but he already knew what I usually needed.

He bought me a twenty-five-pound turkey to stuff and bake. I always remembered our first Thanksgiving in our camper, a small event but memorable. Back then, I found a rice dressing recipe that we both preferred, and I have made it ever since.

I was busy at work before the weekend, but Bill got down to the business of preparing for our dinner. When I came home, the house always smelled so wonderful. He made several of his traditional pumpkin pies, adding his special touch to make them especially delicious. His pecan pies were also a family favorite. He didn't just sprinkle pecans on the pies, but carefully arranged pecan halves around the top before baking them. And he made his "famous" chocolate brownies, another family choice.

On Saturday, I simmered a small turkey in a large pot of water for several hours, until the tender meat fell off the bone. The kitchen smelled good enough to make a stomach rumble. After the broth cooled, I removed the bones and meat and chopped them into small pieces to add to the dressing and turkey gravy.

When making my rice dressing, I made enough to stuff the turkey and fill a large baking pan. I added chopped onions and celery, spices, turkey meat, and broth to the dressing and gravy. My dressing and the gravy took the place of mashed potatoes and gravy for our dinner. We added a variety of stovetop vegetables and tossed salads to the dinner, too.

While the dressing and gravy cooked, I made and baked two loaves of yeast bread. I always made enough dough to make a large pan of cinnamon rolls, which I covered with my special lemon-flavored icing. I had made cinnamon rolls since we were married, and our family expected them.

The Smell ... So Good.

I cooked a small goose for our first Thanksgiving dinner. After that, I cooked a stuffed turkey. In the early years, the turkey was small, and it cooked in three hours. As our family grew, the turkeys became bigger and cooked longer. Eventually, I had to get up by 4 a.m. to put the turkey in the oven.

Improving on that chore, I discovered a different plan. I set the oven to 350 degrees the evening before our dinner. I cooked the turkey for one hour, then turned the oven down to 212 degrees and left the turkey to cook overnight.

The next morning, it was fully cooked and beautifully browned. And the smell... so good.

I removed it from the oven, covered it with a towel to keep it warm until dinnertime. Then I turned the oven temperature back up to use it for other baking.

The Business of Eating.

To eat our family dinner, we used the formal dining room on the floor above the kitchen. The kids and grandkids set the large table with my beautiful china dinnerware, Fostoria crystal, and silverware. Then we carried the stuffed turkey on its enormous platter and the many other foods up to the side buffet. Quite a process.

We could seat twelve at the extended dining table, and four of the teenage grandkids sat at a small side table. Before we sat down to eat, we gathered around the table, holding hands. With bowed heads and closed eyes, we thanked God for the food, our many blessings, and for each other.

Bill stood by his captain's chair at the head of the table. As his tradition, he carved the turkey. We let the teenagers fill their plates first before the rest of us sat down. After that, we began passing the turkey and other dishes around the table.

It didn't seem to take long for everyone to sit back and talk about how full they were. Yet, somehow, we all made room to eat the variety of desserts and my cinnamon rolls throughout the rest of the day.

Good Day, But Sad Too.

Later, we all stacked the dishes, cleared the table, and carried it all back downstairs to the dishwasher. This working time together was also special to us, as we continued visiting and catching up with our lives.

By late afternoon, everyone began talking about going home. It always made me a bit sad, but there would be many other times together. Bill and I wouldn't let them leave, though, until we loaded them down with leftovers, especially the desserts. And they couldn't leave without getting lots of hugs and kisses and reminders of being together again for Christmas.

Since I would return to work the next day, I wanted to get all the dishes put away. But Bill came in and said, "Just sit down and relax. I'll finish it all tomorrow."

I let him, and we went to the family room and settled into our matching recliners to watch the fireplace, exhausted. It didn't take long for us to retire to our bedroom for a much-needed good night's sleep. I would have a busy week ahead at work, and I had agreed to work on Thanksgiving Day with the other nursing staff.

Christmas Preparations.

During that busy work week, I made the nursing staff schedule for December. I had already told them I planned to work Christmas Day. It was not difficult to schedule staff for the day. Some staff asked to have Christmas Eve off and work Christmas Day, at double the pay. Others planned their Christmas celebration around their usual shift, receiving double-time pay for working both days.

While dealing with my workload, I also started making plans for our family Christmas get-together. I set my many boxes of decorations out on the bed in our extra downstairs bedroom, but we needed a tree.

The Saturday after Thanksgiving, I persuaded Bill to take me in his pickup to the Christmas tree farm to get a live tree. He knew I would take the truck myself if he didn't go. Our ceilings were not as high in this house, only eight feet. I found a nice, thick, seven-foot tree and thought it was the prettiest one on the farm. We loaded it in the truck and even carried it inside the house by ourselves.

We got it set up in a sturdy stand he made. I used a ladder to string lights around the very full tree. Then it took me several days after work to arrange and rearrange the beautiful ornaments we had collected over the years. Decorating the tree always made me think of years past.

Because I was working full time—and sometimes more— it was a challenge to do everything I planned. As usual, it was "Bill to the rescue." He did the grocery shopping, cooking, cleaning, and laundry. We made a good team.

Christmas shopping was my area. I did most of it from catalogs, which saved much time. As I had done since our first Christmas together, I ordered boxes of chocolate-covered cherries, hard and filled candy, and cashew nuts from the Sears Christmas catalog. The packages came to our house by mail. I wrapped the gifts and put them under the tree. The sight of the growing pile made me eager for sharing them with everyone.

We share more than presents; we shared goodies. Our family always wanted a variety of homemade candies, especially fudge and divinity, this time of year. I also made candied special fruit, added nuts, and made holiday fruitcakes as I had done for years. Bill and everyone expected them. But our kids and families preferred his pecan pies and delectable brownies.

Holiday Time at Work.

Besides the Christmas preparations happening at home, I had to deal with busy times at the nursing home. In early December, company owners returned. They knew we had nursing staff in place and were stable without using agency help. The nursing staff received the optimal wages they deserved since the company was now making a profit.

I had been with the company for three months, and it was typical to evaluate nursing staff at that time. If merited, they usually gave them a raise. The management gave me an excellent review and a generous raise.

I felt good about that, and about getting the facility ready for the holidays. The residents and employees were excited about the upcoming Christmas holidays.

Cooking, Eating ... Oh, my!

The weekend of our family Christmas get-together, Bill did our grocery shopping. He made sure I had everything

I needed to make my special dishes and desserts. He got a sizeable boneless ham for dinner this time. Since we didn't do turkey and dressing, we would make mashed potatoes and gravy, and candied sweet potatoes.

On Saturday, we kept the oven going all day, making all the anticipated foods. Bill baked his pecan pies and brownies. I made loaves of yeast bread and iced cinnamon rolls. The cooked sweet potatoes were candied and ready to bake the following day.

The next morning, Bill awakened me from a deep sleep. He already had the fireplace going and Christmas carols playing non-stop, and he had breakfast waiting on the table for us. What a wonderful start to the day.

After enjoying coffee to get me started, Connie and I peeled and cooked potatoes. As they boiled, I made the gravy to go with them. We cut and chopped lettuce and other ingredients for a large, healthy tossed salad. And there were peas, green beans, and corn to cook to fill out the dinner menu. Again, the kitchen filled with the smells of baking ham and so many other wonderful, tempting dishes.

By mid-morning, our other families arrived with presents to add under the Christmas tree. The grandkids—and some adults—were eager to open the gifts, but dinner came first.

We set the large dining room table and the grandkids' side table as we had for Thanksgiving dinner with my fine china, crystal, and silverware. It was quite a task carrying all the many drinks, ham, side dishes, and desserts upstairs. As before, the ham was placed by Bill's plate at the head of the table for him to slice.

Before we could eat, we gathered around the table, joined hands, bowed our heads, and thanked God for sending Baby

Jesus. We thanked him for the food, our family, and so many blessings.

While the kids were small, Bill had not allowed them to talk as they ate. Now, we all talked, laughed, and visited as we enjoyed the meal and time together.

Appreciating Family Time.

Tummies full, our grandkids let us know it was time to open presents. As we had done for many Christmas get-togethers, someone read the poem "The Night Before Christmas."

With everyone seated around the tree, Bill and I handed out our gifts first, starting with the youngest. It pleased us to watch as our family opened the presents.

As our family grew in numbers, it became too much for them to buy gifts for everyone. So, we settled on a game which we all enjoyed, one which many families and groups do. We each brought one small, secret present in a gift bag without a name on it. Then we each drew a number from a hat.

The person who drew number one chose any bag they wanted and opened it. If the gift was something they didn't particularly like, too bad. The person with number two then chose a bag, or they could "steal" from number one. In that case, number one, chose a new gift bag. Choosing a bag or stealing from someone kept going until everyone had a present. Each present could only be "stolen" three times. The game usually lasted about two hours, with lots of good-natured teasing and laughing.

While the presents game continued, we also snacked on leftovers from dinner, cinnamon rolls, and ham sandwiches on the homemade bread. Plus, the desserts and candies.

As evening drew near, our families began talking about going home. Most of us had to work the next day. We worked together to stack the dishes and carry them downstairs to the kitchen. We bagged the leftover foods and desserts for our kids to take with them. No one left the house hungry.

They went home after being hugged and kissed and wished a Merry Christmas and a blessed New Year. Bill and I felt so fortunate to have our family members with us for the Christmas celebration. And, as always, we were exhausted after the busy day. We retired to get a much-needed sleep.

Christmas at Work.

Bill awakened me the following morning to an early breakfast. I braced myself to head to work for the week before Christmas, knowing it would be quite a week.

Residents, their families, and the staff were celebrating the season. Family members had decorated the residents' rooms. The housekeeping, laundry, kitchen, and nursing staff helped put Christmas trees and decorations throughout the nursing home. It was all bright and colorful. To make the season joyful, we invited in musical groups from the community. Groups, including school children, walked the halls and sang Christmas carols all week.

As planned, I worked both Christmas Eve and Christmas Day. The nursing staff showed up as scheduled. We enjoyed spending the holiday with the residents and their families.

A Special Tree Lives On.

When I got home from work on Christmas Day, Bill had a fire burning in the fireplace in our family room. Such a welcoming sight. He spent the day with our families and came home to prepare a delicious supper for us. Wanting to relax after a long day, we sat in our easy chairs, with a full plate of food, and ate while watching TV.

Work after Christmas Day was busy and tiring. It was a week until New Year's Day. I usually waited until then, or sometimes later, to take our Christmas tree down, but I had been thinking about the chore.

Family Christmas tree

As I hurried home one day and down to the family room, it shocked me to see the tree already gone. Bill had removed the ornaments and tree lights and neatly boxed them all up. He told me he dragged the tree out back and chopped it up to burn the limbs and branches in our fireplace.

"I got tired of vacuuming the tree needles out of our carpet." Then he firmly added, "No more live Christmas trees. I'm not vacuuming any more needles out of our carpet."

I knew he meant it. But I had enjoyed a live tree for over fifty years.

I noticed a craft store I frequented was selling discounted artificial Christmas trees. One day, on my way home from work before New Year's Eve, I stopped there to price their trees. Most of them were small and thin. I continued looking and found a large, beautiful six-foot tree for $100. The original price was $400. I bought it and the store employees loaded it in my car trunk.

Back home, Bill smiled in approval, unloaded the boxed tree, and stored it in the garage. A happy man.

This Christmas tree became a family treasure, and we used it for many years at Lake Waltanna. When we later moved to town, we set it up in our downstairs family room. We left the tree up for several years, changing the decorations for the season, especially for Easter. When I moved to an apartment, the tree was too large for me to use. I gave it to my grandson, his wife, and daughter. The tree "Lives On."

Chapter Nine
LIFE CHANGES

Quieter Than Normal.

There were busy days at work after the holidays. Our Director of Nursing (DON) and other department heads were planning for the upcoming annual State nursing home survey. If we got written up for many infractions, they allowed us time to correct them. We didn't want any problems.

I worked a lot of overtime, mostly by choice, to ensure that our nursing department provided standard and quality care. As always, Bill made sure I didn't need to worry about housework when I got home. He had supper ready and waiting, which I greatly appreciated.

This time of year, his schedule changed. He was not mowing lawns, working on his or other's cars, or cleaning the pool. Most days, it was too cold to do his long walk around the lake. And we seldom had guests because our families and friends were back in their daily routines.

Instead of his other routine, Bill spent extra time grocery shopping and visiting with employees he had become acquainted with. He took time to also make his tasty beef stew and kept large containers of it at the ready in our freezer. I suspected family and friends who stopped in for a visit came hoping to eat some of that stew. It seemed as if he was busy and enjoying himself.

One mid-January Saturday morning, it was stormy

outside, not a good day for getting out. We didn't want to go anywhere and stayed home relaxing and appreciating a quiet time. Bill had already taken care of the household chores and the cooking. I had some free time to knit on a sweater project.

When suppertime came, we settled into our recliners to watch our usual TV shows. Bill's favorite one was the Grand Ole Opry, which I also liked. We ate more of his beef stew and his special treat, the family-loved brownies. While it continued being stormy outside, we kept warm and toasty by the fireplace.

Bill was a quiet man, but he seemed more subdued than normal. After we finished eating, he did the dishes, never leaving a dirty dish in the sink, unlike me. When that chore was done, we retired for the evening, knowing we would get around the next morning to attend church.

Everything In Me Froze.

Usually, I didn't get up until Bill woke me. I woke on my own this morning. I glanced at the clock: eight o'clock. Looking over at Bill, I found him lying on his back, eyes closed, and his hands folded over his chest. But I sensed he was awake.

He glanced at me and closed his eyes again. "I just don't know why I should have to go on living."

Stunned, I couldn't talk for a moment. Everything in me froze. I couldn't breathe.

Then I recovered enough to raise up on my knees beside him to shake his shoulder. Sobbing, I uttered words I had never used before. Words that cannot or should not be repeated here.

Still crying in distress, I sat back on my heels. I reminded him how our kids and I had worried about him for long months after his heart attack and triple bypass surgery. How we had prayed he would not leave us for a long, long time.

As he lay there just listening, I reminded him how well he had recovered because of the skilled doctors and healthcare providers. I told him we had so much more now than we had ever dreamed of and should be grateful for it. Many people our age didn't have enough to eat, or a good place to live. We were so fortunate.

He continued to just lay there.

I sat for a moment on the side of the bed, frustrated and scared for him. Finally, I got up, put on my warm robe, and went to cook breakfast, needing time to absorb all of this. As I cooked, I heard Bill shaving as he did each morning.

After a while, he walked into the kitchen dressed for church in his suit. Perfectly normal.

Without speaking about what had happened, we both gave simple smiles and sat down to eat. Afterward, I went to dress for church, trying to act normal as well.

He was his usual self at church, greeting our friends, shaking hands, and sometimes hugging. For now, we focused on everything there and enjoyed the service and the singing. Then, as was our tradition, we went to our favorite restaurant for Sunday dinner.

The weather was stormy again, so we went home to settle into our comfy recliners. The warmth from the fireplace comforted us even more while we watched TV. The routine was relaxing, but there was an uneasiness between us.

Underlying Tension.

Bill remained silent about what we had said earlier. I hadn't stopped thinking about it. But I was reluctant to say anything, not wanting to rant at him again.

By late afternoon, I couldn't keep quiet anymore. "Are you okay? Do you want me to stay home with you tomorrow?" I asked, in concern.

"Oh no," he said in that quiet yet firm way he had. "You need to go to work. I'll be okay."

Inside, I worried, but I didn't want to press him. Yet I knew I would remain concerned and watchful.

I was still anxious when I went to work the next day. The following two days at work were busy, but Bill was always on my mind.

Bill's Surprising News.

Returning home from work Wednesday evening, the roads were icy and made me nervous. Bill seemed relieved that I made it home safe and sound. As typical, we sat down to eat the meal he had prepared. I remained worried about him but didn't know what to say.

"I signed up to deliver Meals on Wheels today," he said between bites.

I stopped eating, blinking at him. The quiet announcement was a surprise, a good one.

"I signed up to deliver meals two days a week." He explained the drivers were offered gas money, but he chose not to accept it. He relayed what I already knew; that the meals were prepared by Senior Services of Wichita and delivered by volunteer drivers.

What a blessing! With that decision, his life was about to change... our lives would change.

Bill started delivering meals and then he talked to me about the older adults he met on his route. They didn't have their own transportation. Some of them didn't have families or friends close by. Many of them told him he was the only person they saw all week. All of what they shared with him touched him.

Volunteers couldn't go inside the client's home and he respected that rule. Often the client would reach out to hold his hand, needing that simple human contact. With his big heart, he told me how he would stand there and hold their hand and visit with them for several minutes. But he couldn't stay long because he had a number of clients on his route.

Until this experience, Bill had not known there were so many lonely and hungry older people in the community. After talking with them and learning about their many needs, he often shared their concerns with the social workers at the organization. He did this so the people would get follow-up attention from their healthcare workers.

I Missed the Signs.

This had me thinking about how depressed Bill was after the holidays. Healthcare workers are aware of a symptom and diagnosis known as Post Holiday Depression. Nurses also knew about it. But sometimes we didn't recognize the symptoms in our own family members or those close to us.

I was one of those who had missed the signs and felt bad for it.

Bill continued volunteering with the Meals on Wheels program for over ten years, unless we traveled. He became a friend with many of the older adults on his route. His time delivering those meals to people in need positively changed our lives. It helped give him a special reason to "go on living."

Life could not get any better for us. Our kids and grandkids often visited. Bill delivered his meals twice a week when the weather allowed. He took comfort in knowing that they had backup meals on hand when he couldn't get to them. But he looked forward to seeing his "friends" almost as much as bringing their food.

Busy Times at Work.

By the middle of February, I had missed no work, even though the roads were often icy and slick, challenging to travel on. Our nursing staff was reliable, performing well and meeting scheduling expectations. I was content that we were prepared for the upcoming annual State nursing home survey expected by the end of the month.

The surveyors were in our residents' home for a week. They evaluated the cleanliness of our home provided by the housekeeping and laundry staff. They assessed the quality of food preparation and documentation of each resident's needs. And they observed and evaluated the quality of care provided by the nursing staff. This included processing the doctors' orders and follow-through with medications and other interventions.

The completed survey showed we had only minor write-ups, which were quickly corrected. Overall, it had been a good—even excellent—survey, and I was very happy. The outcome also pleased our out-of-state company officials who had been there during the survey.

Everything Running Smoothly.

Our DON had not taken a vacation in over two years. Relieved that the State survey was over and had gone well, she took her vacation. I was comfortable acting as DON in her absence.

I was ready to work there indefinitely. I had become friends with many of the staff in all departments and with our residents and their families. It felt like my life at work and at home with Bill and our families was running smoother than it had for years.

About a week after the State survey, I got a phone call from a professional friend made while working on my master's degree. She had been on the faculty then but was now an official with the State, conducting nursing home surveys.

After the initial greeting, she said, "There is a DON position open in a large nursing home outside Wichita. I want you to apply for it. The administrator is expecting a call from you." My friend explained she had recommended me because of the nursing home's superior survey. An added incentive was that there would be a significant pay increase. I told her I would think about it.

This nursing home was fifty miles from where we lived,

but I was now driving many miles through traffic. Many questions ran through my mind. What would Bill think? Did I want to change workplaces? I needed to talk it over with Bill.

That evening I waited until after supper with him to mention the matter. I told him about the phone call and the offer.

He looked somewhat surprised. "Is that what you want to do?"

Time to Think.

"I'm not sure." We didn't discuss the issue further. I needed to think it over. I liked my current job.

A few days later, I got another call from my friend who worked for the State. She asked me why I had not applied for the position. The management there was expecting me to call and make an appointment for an interview. She gave me their phone number and urged me to make contact.

Again, I talked about it to Bill. Again, he asked me if I wanted to consider the change. He said he would support me in whatever decision I made. I called the nursing home and made the appointment. Bill drove me there.

After we made introductions, I handed the administrator my resume and sat down in her office for the interview.

She didn't even look at. She laid it on her desk and looked straight at me. "You have the DON position if you want it. I know about the excellent survey at your current facility. And I know it was primarily due to your management of the nursing staff and your work with the other departments."

I appreciated her kind words and listened as she told me that this home had just received a poor survey. They needed a DON with my skills to get adequate and quality staffing in place. The facility was using an agency for about one-fourth of their staffing. Some of the agency staff had worked there for several years. She also explained that this home was church owned with about one hundred residents.

Bill joined us while she gave me a tour of the two-story facility. As we walked, I thought about how he had said I should make my decision and that he would support it. We always supported each other, and that was important to me.

Decision Made.

When we returned to the office, while Bill waited close by, I made my decision. I accepted the DON position and signed the contract to begin work in one month. The pay increase was not why I took the job, but it didn't hurt that I nearly doubled my current salary and increased my benefits. Bill was pleased with my choice, but I knew he would have backed me either way.

My current DON returned from her vacation a week later. I waited until she was back a few days before giving her my two-week notice of resignation. She was visibly surprised, annoyed, and upset. She asked me what I was going to do now. I explained about getting a contract for a DON position at the other nursing home.

She was unfriendly toward me for the remaining two weeks I worked there. I later learned that she had applied for the same position while on her vacation. Hearing that I had taken the job was how she found out she didn't get it. I believe she had hoped to get the new position and tell me that she was leaving, and then I could have her current job.

First Time in Charge.

My new position as Director of Nursing in the other nursing home was the first official time in my nursing career that I was in charge. I would assure quality care by the nursing staff for our residents, and I looked forward to the responsibilities.

The retiring DON gave me two weeks of orientation to become acquainted with the nursing staff and the other employees. She showed me the schedules and paperwork I would be responsible for and reminded that the position could be an overwhelming effort. I believed I was up to the challenge. And I took this time to get to know most of the one hundred residents and their families.

During orientation, I observed the basic needs of the residents were being met. Still, the quality of care for each resident could, should, and would be improved on my watch. I also made note of the several staff members from an agency, both CNAs and nurses.

My office—the first one in my career—was down a long hallway from the residents and the dining rooms. I observed the current DON wore high heels and dress clothes. In contrast, I wore what I considered nice casual clothes and an attractive, colorful lab coat. She told me I could "dress up" if I wanted to, but this was my preference for work clothes.

My First Changes.

While reviewing the nursing staff records, I discovered they were being grossly underpaid, and most had not received a raise in years. The CNAs were being paid less than $5.00 an hour, meager pay for that time. All the staff had paid healthcare insurance. Some agency staff were being paid double our staff's wages and had worked there for many years. Based on standard wages, they allowed me to nearly double the wages of our home's long-time employees.

With the nursing staff soon stabilized, and frequent, chronic turnovers decreased, I no longer had to use the agency. One agency CNA had worked there for a long time. I told her she would need to become one of our home's employees if she continued with us.

"No, I won't do that," she told me. A couple of weeks later, she came to me and hired on with us because of our benefits and an increase in wages.

My primary responsibility was getting quality staffing in place and providing the support they needed to care for our residents. One of the most essential functions I provided was the monthly schedule. Scheduling every other weekend off for the nursing staff allowed them to plan their work and home lives to meet their family's needs. Both licensed and certified nursing workers began coming to me to apply for various nursing positions without me having to advertise. This meant I could hire the highly qualified staff we needed.

A Hug is Good Medicine.

I believed it was important to get to know each employee and resident of our nursing home. When I arrived at work each morning, the residents were in the two dining rooms for breakfast. I greeted each of our nursing staff there by name. As I became acquainted with the residents, I greeted them by name, too, and helped serve their breakfasts.

Soon I noticed some of them had little family or visitors. Believing that familiar saying, "A hug is good medicine," I often gave them a hug along with their meal. Sometimes there were tears in the resident's eyes, sometimes in mine as well.

With adequate staffing no longer an issue, I began conducting in-service meetings monthly to assess the quality of care for the residents. It helped improve my communication with them.

Efforts Appreciated.

Time passed quickly. By late summer, it was time for my ninety-day evaluation. We now had a new, just-out-of-college administrator. This was his first nursing home position.

We greeted each other and sat down in his office for the interview. He questioned the cost of some changes I had made and my reason for them, which I confidently explained. And he acknowledged that our home was now making a profit, a primary concern for him. At the end of the interview, he gave me a generous raise, much appreciated.

The frequent volunteers from our church and community

were also pleased with the noticeable improvement in nursing staff and resident care. They had known some of our residents before they came to our home. We discussed the needs of those who did not have close family or friends to visit them. The volunteers arranged for various individuals and groups to come in and entertain our residents, which everyone loved.

With the coming of Christmas, our volunteers and family members decorated our residents' rooms, the dining rooms, and hallways. They put up colorful, festive decorations and several lighted Christmas trees. Appreciated by both staff and residents.

As in my prior positions, I would work both Thanksgiving and Christmas Day. I had no problem with scheduling staff on those days, maybe because I was there. I know it helped that they got holiday pay, which I did not.

Outside of work, our kids and their families continued our tradition of getting together the weekends before Thanksgiving and Christmas Day. I enjoyed my time at work both days, just as I had in the past. Also, as had become tradition, Bill would spend those days at our kids' homes.

To Benefit Our Residents.

Everything we did at our nursing home benefited the residents. Part of that included making sure we provided our nursing staff the support they needed to do their jobs. One effort along that line included my promoting one of our charge nurses to Assistant Director of Nursing (ADON). She assisted with taking and implementing doctors' orders.

The ADON and I worked with the doctors and charge nurses. We evaluated and changed medications with the doctor's approval. The doctors appreciated our increased input. We also talked with our residents and their family members about order changes, and they noticed the improvement in the lives and wellbeing of the residents.

By the middle of March, it was time for the surveyors to come for our annual State nursing home survey. It had been a year since their last survey before I began working here. My help with changes was why they had recruited me for the DON position. With the positive improvements we had made, I knew we were ready for their visit.

The surveyors came to observe and assess all our departments. Because it had the most deficiencies in the last survey, they closely evaluated the nursing department. We supported and assisted them in any way we could.

After being in our home for a week, the surveyors gave the results to our administrator and me, the DON. We received only one write-up. A nurse had crushed a pill, per doctor's orders. According to the surveyor, she did not give the resident all the residue (dust) when she mixed the crushed pill into applesauce. We assured the surveyors we would instruct her to always administer carefully the fully crushed med. However, we wondered if the surveyors were searching for something to write up.

Our employees—especially the nursing department, the residents, and their families celebrated for several days with extra snacks and treats.

Success at Work.

I had now worked at this nursing home for a year and was proud of what we had accomplished. The administrator called me into his office for my annual evaluation. We went over his list of questions for my assessment, and then he expressed his pleasure with the outcome of the State survey. Smiling, he gave me a raise, always appreciated.

We had begun scheduling one-year paid vacations for our nurses and CNAs. Our nursing department had several part-time and PRN employees. So, there was adequate staffing to schedule vacations when they qualified.

Now it was time for me to think about taking my annual two-week paid vacation. I had never worked in one place long enough to take a yearly vacation. With our reliable ADON in place and stable and dependable nursing staff available, I could do it.

Time Away.

After busy days at work, it was time for Bill and me to take a paid vacation. We had taken many great trips over the years throughout the country. We visited historic sites, including former presidents' homes. I had heard about Eureka Springs, Arkansas, a resort area with numerous folk and gospel stage shows and was excited to visit there.

Bill loaded our camper with needed linens and the refrigerator and cabinets with food. All I had to do was add my clothes. What a sweet man to handle so many extra details for us.

We enjoyed the scenic drive with the area's rolling hills and beautiful foliage. Wichita has its own beauty, but this was far different. And we enjoyed taking in the shows and dining on local foods.

But what I wanted to see the most was their internationally known The Great Passion Play. The settings, scenes, and costumes were well researched and authentic. They presented the reenactment of the last week of the life of Jesus Christ each evening in spring, summer, and fall when the weather permitted.

One evening, I suggested to Bill that we go to the play. He was not interested. I silently refused to take "No" for an answer and wanted to see it, even if I had to go by myself. However, a few days later, he reluctantly agreed to go with me.

The outdoor setting for the play was on a long, naturally sloping hillside. We sat down before the play started on seats amongst the hundreds of bench seats with backs set in the hillside. The ground leveled off at the bottom of the hill, where replicas of ancient buildings, dirt roads, and streets were laid out. We watched horses, cattle, camels, sheep, pigs, cats, dogs, and chickens mill around. Children played games. Men and women walked around. Men on horses and horse-drawn carriages seemed to move with a purpose. It was all so real.

Bill appeared disinterested, but I found it all fascinating.

As darkness came, the play began with well-lighted action scenes. We saw the performers speaking and heard the clear sounds of their recorded voices. The first scene was of The Last Supper in the upper room with Jesus and His disciples. They fully presented each scene with lighting and sound.

On the Edge of His Seat.

Finally, Bill noticed what was happening and listened. Soon he was on the edge of his seat, holding onto the back of the bench in front of him, taking it all in.

After that first scene, the play proceeded to the trial, the horrible, realistic crucifixion scene, and the burial in the tomb. The last scene was of the women finding the empty tomb and Jesus' ascension into Heaven. I felt as though I had been there when it happened. I had never been so emotionally touched by a performance.

The Great Passion Play lasted over two hours. But the enormous effects of it are still in my mind and heart, reminding me of the sacrifice of our Wonderful Savior, Jesus, and what he did for me... for all of us.

It had been a wonderful week in Eureka Springs, a memorable one. Yet Bill and I were ready to head home. The camper was fun, but we hoped to have some time for ourselves back in our comfortable home before family and friends knew we were back from vacation.

New Problem at Work.

I felt refreshed after our time away on vacation with Bill. Still, I was ready to get back to my work as DON and plan for another good year.

My first day back, the employees, nursing staff, and residents made me feel welcome as I greeted them at breakfast. Hugging some of our residents was always a pleasure. It was a nice homecoming.

Our ADON smiled and told me she was ready to turn the responsibilities back to me. She reported that all had gone well while I was on vacation. But there was one issue with a CNA just out of high school last spring.

They had adopted the young woman when she was sixteen and had been in and out of foster homes all her life prior to that. Her new mother loved her, and it pleased her when the girl found something she liked and wanted to do. She completed the CNA classes, and we hired her full-time.

After going through the two-week orientation, she had been working for us for several weeks and the residents had quickly accepted her, and she loved caring for them. Now I heard from other CNAs that she was not changing her residents' soiled briefs. One CNA, in particular, came to me and reported that the young woman had put a resident back to bed without changing their soiled, disposable brief.

When I confronted her, she broke down and started sobbing. "I love the residents, but I just can't change a soiled brief without getting sick to my stomach."

I felt sorry for her, but this was part of her job. I called her mother and relayed what had happened and what her daughter had said. It was difficult, but I explained her daughter could not continue working in the CNA position. This disappointed the mother because her daughter loved the residents.

A Happy Ending.

I had an idea that might work for the young woman and for us. A CNA could become an Activity Director (AD) by taking classes for the position. I called the mother in and met with her and her daughter. They already understood the young woman couldn't continue in the job because of the problem with changing briefs.

I explained the responsibilities of an AD: scheduling games, entertainment, and activities for the residents. When I asked if she would be interested in taking the necessary classes and working in that capacity, she answered, "Yes!"

We already had an AD, but I told her we could use an Assistant AD (AAD) for our many residents.

My next step was to talk the situation over with our administrator. He agreed and allowed the young woman to resign. She took the classes, and we hired her back as a full-time AAD. It pleased the residents to see her back again, and it was a happy ending for all of us.

One Toothless Grin.

I continued to hold monthly nursing in-service meetings with each shift that fall. It gave me the chance to become closely acquainted with them, and notice that some of our CNAs were dedicated to learning more to improve their quality of care for our residents. I encouraged them to consider continuing their education and become a licensed nurse. When they wished, I helped get loans and scholarships, so some of them went on to become licensed nurses. We never had a problem replacing the CNAs.

Our residents well liked a CNA on the day shift and she seemed content with her job. I thought she might be interested in furthering her education and advancing her career to becoming licensed. One day at work, I asked her about it.

She looked directly at me and said, "My parents didn't appreciate me. My teachers didn't appreciate me. My husband doesn't appreciate me. My kids don't appreciate me. But one toothless grin from one of these residents makes my day. I'm doing just what I want to do."

Humbled and proud of her, I said, "I'm glad you are here. We need more CNAs like you. Please stay here and work for us as long as you want."

She nodded. "Not many people can say that they are doing just what they want to do."

Our nursing home had become a choice place of employment. Wages were the best, so staffing was stable. I easily managed the changes in staff sometimes needed, with part-time staffing in place to cover vacations. With this situation, I kept my hours at forty hours a week, as my DON salary specified.

Life Beyond Work.

Bill and I could now spend our quiet evenings together. After eating his delectable meals or snacking on them later, we sat in our recliners and watched TV in front of the fire in the fireplace.

Our grown kids were busy with their work and lives, and some of our grandkids were now teenagers. Time passed so quickly. But they still found time for us and enjoyed the swimming pool as long as the weather allowed. The grandkids knew their Papa would always have hot soups, snacks, and desserts ready for them.

We were still active in our church. Bill continued cooking for church dinners and swapping recipes with the other cooks. He was also on the Finance Committee and the Maintenance Committee, and he mowed the church lawn for years.

There were three retired ministers and their wives at our church. None of them wanted to teach the Bible study classes on Sunday morning. So, I volunteered. Our denomination didn't officially allow women to teach men, but the ministers agreed—even asked me to do so.

The women of our church sponsored our teenage girls in studying both foreign and home missions. I worked with the girls doing charitable work for those in need in their schools and our community. They liked to meet at our house for pool parties and slumber parties.

Again, the holidays were upon us. And, as usual, our family celebrated them on the Sunday before each holiday. With the continual addition of grandkids, our get-togethers became more exciting each year with lots of little ones.

Sliding Out of Control.

With the holidays behind us, I focused on work. I drove fifty miles each way, and each trip took about an hour. It meant that I spent two hours each day driving to work and back. In the wintertime, they usually cleared the roads of ice and snow. I didn't let the weather stop me until...

One day when I was at work, it started snowing mixed with freezing rain. With snowplows working and the roads being salted, they seemed passable with care. Heading south on the main highway, I was within a few miles of home. It had taken me well over an hour to get that far, and I wasn't home yet.

An eighteen-wheeler slowly headed north in the lane next to me. I hit an ice-glazed spot on the road, and my car started sliding out of control. My heart pounded as I realized it was heading toward the back wheels of the trailer.

My car got hit on the right front fender in front of the passenger's door.

It threw me from the driver's seat into the passenger seat, hitting my right shoulder against the door. (This was before seat belts and crash bags.) The truck driver dragged my car a short distance before he could get stopped. I was able to climb back across to the driver's seat, get out, stand, and walk.

Cars were stopping, Drivers ran toward me in concern. Noticing that I was in a daze, someone offered to call an ambulance. I told them, "No." I didn't want to make a fuss.

We heard sirens and the Highway Patrol showed up.

There were no cell phones then. But the Highway Patrolman called Bill for me.

And He Was There.

He was there in a few minutes; that's how close I was to getting home. I assured him I was okay, and he carefully walked me to his pickup to head home.

Bill held me close as we walked through our front door. I'm sure he noticed I was still traumatized and shaking. I realized that as bad as the accident was, I could have been seriously injured... or worse. He knew me well enough to know I was in pain, even if I didn't say anything.

After taking some over-the-counter pain pills, a big, hot bowl of his beef stew comforted me. Then I took a long soak in our whirlpool tub.

I fell asleep quickly that night, but morning came too soon, with the pain. Bill tried to persuade me to call in sick, but I refused. My car was totaled, but we had a second car besides the pickup. I took more pain pills, got dressed, ate a good breakfast, and drove to work.

Before the accident, I had already questioned whether I wanted to continue the long drive each day to work. I had received calls and letters from other nursing home administrators from facilities much closer to home wanting to hire me as their DON. The administrators had usually experienced a poor State survey and wanted help to correct it, to stabilize their staff and help them financially. Their offers often included a generous increase in salary.

A few days later, Bill and I discussed the advantages of my working closer to home. Besides the safety advantages, there were the savings in gas and wear and tear on my car.

Over Sixty and Options.

I wanted to stay in my present position until after our annual State nursing home survey. I did, and we had another excellent survey, thanks to the great staff in all departments.

When considering the timing of my resignation, I waited until my annual evaluation. Again, my administrator gave me a good review and a raise in salary. Yet I had made an important decision and gave him my two weeks' notice, which he understood. I left, receiving my vacation pay with the increase.

Before leaving, the administrator and staff, the residents, and their families held a going-away party and wished me well. I made many friendships there that have lasted a lifetime.

I had many options for my future in nursing, even though I was over sixty years old now. Before deciding on a new position, I took some time to relax and enjoy our home by the lake and time alone with Bill.

Chapter Ten
THE NEXT PHASE

What to Do Next.

It was time for me to decide how and where I would use my nursing degree in the future. I had many opportunities and offers in nursing homes for my specialized area of practice in gerontological nursing. This was an exciting time, and I wanted to choose wisely.

Reaching Older Adults.

A nurse friend from Wichita State University asked if I would be interested in consulting for healthcare workers in a small town west of Wichita. This appealed to me, and I agreed to meet with nurses, doctors, and other healthcare workers in their large community hospital.

Under my leadership and working together, we designed a plan of service to reach older adults in the community. The plan involved wellness, prevention, early intervention, and home health services. The goal was to keep these adults well and living in their homes as long as possible.

The community's local news media informed the residents of our program. They encouraged older residents to visit their doctors regularly for preventive care, reducing their need to be hospitalized or go to a nursing home.

There would be times, though, when someone needed

to be admitted to the hospital. When dismissed back to their home, the nurses and doctors would follow up with interventions until the patient was stable. Because of the increased services in place, the patient could sometimes be dismissed sooner.

If the patient was not well enough to return home after hospital dismissal, they would discharge them to rehab for follow-up care. Or they would go to a nursing home. Some of them could later return safely to their homes to a nurse's care and home health as needed.

The program worked well for the small community. A few weeks of increased services of preventive practices and early intervention by nurses and doctors proved beneficial. Hospital and nursing home admissions declined, pleasing everyone.

They paid me well for my consultation work and services with the team and I could have continued with them if I wished. But the increased mileage and approaching bad weather concerned Bill and me.

Closer to Home.

Other options came up. I moved to another nursing position much closer to home.

I responded to an offer I had for a DON position near our home. When the administrator interviewed me, he explained the need for improvements there. As with the other facilities I had worked with, they had a poor annual State nursing home survey that fall. They needed the interventions I had applied before. I accepted the position.

As always, my primary concern was scheduling qualified and adequate nursing staff until it was stable. I soon became aware that over half of the CNAs and some licensed staff were agency staff. Most agency staff were qualified, but their pay per person cost to our home was much more than we paid our staff.

While working on our November schedule, I had no choice but to use agency staff for November and Thanksgiving Day. Since our family, as usual, met the weekend before, I was free to work on that holiday. Our employees were surprised and pleased about my doing so.

Successful Changes at Work.

I wanted to be free of agency staffing by Christmas. After doing performance evaluations for each of our nursing staff, I met with our administrator. He agreed to give earned increases in wages for our employees, and we were able to discontinue the need for and use of agency staff before Christmas. Some of our nursing staff had worked there for over a year and were delighted with their substantial raise.

Not everything went smoothly, and December proved to be a challenging month for me.

One young couple, husband and wife CNAs, were both good workers. When I approached them about working either Christmas Eve or Christmas Day, the husband said they were going out of town for the holidays and would not be available. That was not acceptable for me, but I continued working on the month's schedule.

The couple came to me when they heard I was going

to work both days. Their plans had changed. They would be available to work when I needed them. They chose to work both days on the day shift. Of course, they received double holiday pay for those days. And, with my plan to work both days, I had no other problems scheduling staff for the Christmas holidays.

Now a Great-Granddaughter.

This year, our family get-together the Sunday before Christmas was more cheerful and exciting than ever. Along with the joy of having grandkids, we now had a great-granddaughter. The gifts and wonderful shared foods were better than ever.

Mission Accomplished.

Back at the nursing home after the holidays, we all worked together to correct the deficiencies of last fall's State survey, the reason they had hired me. Our focus was to provide a safe and secure environment and home for our residents and for our staff.

We were pleased, but not surprised, that the annual State nursing home survey went well this time. There were only minor concerns, which we promptly corrected. I believed my mission here was accomplished.

Our administrator had approved an ADON position. She was a highly qualified RN, but the administrator wanted me to stay with the home. I was, however, being recruited by other nursing homes, offering a pay increase. It was helpful, but that wasn't the only reason for changing positions.

More New DON Positions.

A DON position close to our home was too good to refuse. With the ADON in place to assume my current DON role, I gave my two-week notice of resignation. Before I took the new position, Bill and I took a couple of weeks for vacation and visited our families in Missouri.

Refreshed again, I began my new job in another nursing home. The task ahead for me was much like in my former positions. The departments here worked together to correct the deficiencies of their last survey.

When we had our annual State survey, it went well. As in the last nursing home where I worked, there were only minor infractions, which were quickly corrected. Once more, with all going well, I resigned.

Yet again, another nursing home needed help after receiving a poor survey and made me an offer I couldn't refuse, better pay and benefits. We accomplished the needed improvements over the next few months and were ready for the annual State survey.

A Career Stretch.

While working at that nursing home, I began questioning whether I wanted to continue in a DON position for the rest of my nursing career. For several years, a professor at WSU had encouraged me to become a school nurse. She knew me as a graduate teaching assistant, working with pre-nursing students. She was involved with the Wichita School Nurse profession.

It concerned me that it would be a stretch for me to go from gerontological nursing to being a school nurse. The professor, though, thought I would fit well into school nursing. The school hours would be much less than at a nursing home, and the pay and benefits were better, with a union retirement. Add to that, I would have holidays and summers off.

When I discussed the change with Bill, he was, as always, supportive. As usual, he said, "Go for it!"

The home where I currently worked received an excellent State survey, with only slight infractions that were easily fixed. As before, with all going well there, I resigned.

I applied for the school nurse position, and they hired me because my professor friend had told them about my successes at work. I had several weeks before I started this new job, which allowed me the luxury of just relaxing by the pool and having friends and our families visit us. And Bill and I took a trip to Niagara Falls.

Becoming a School Nurse.

Excited but a bit apprehensive, I began a thorough two-week orientation for my school nursing position. They made me aware of the responsibilities, needs, and concerns I would deal with. I had known school nurses when our kids were in school. Thankfully, a school nurse gave Susan an eye exam in first grade and informed us she needed glasses.

The only full-time school nursing positions available

were far from our home. I was offered and encouraged to work as a much-needed substitute nurse, which I did. I found it a beneficial experience. The first year, I worked in elementary schools throughout the Wichita School District for one or two weeks at a time in each school. I usually chose schools close to home.

An Unfortunate Situation.

One situation in early October remains in my memory because it had such a positive outcome. They had not promoted an eight-year-old girl past first grade. The school staff told me her life story.

The girl's single mother was diagnosed as developmentally and mentally challenged. In her teens, a co-worker had raped her in her workplace, she became pregnant, and delivered a baby girl. The mother was not competent in supporting or caring for her baby. They lived with her parents—the girl's grandparents—who had custody of the child.

Most of the staff knew and talked about the little girl's situation. Knowing about her mother's condition, the consensus was she was not capable of higher learning.

The school nurse had a responsibility to do basic physical assessments of students, especially those struggling with their schoolwork. As I assessed the girl's basic hearing, I became concerned that her hearing was severely limited.

I talked with her grandparents, and they expressed their concern about her vision. She was pulling her chair up close to watch TV. I arranged a vision examination for her. She qualified for prescription glasses, and they provided them without cost to her grandparents.

Still concerned about the girl's hearing, I arranged a hearing exam for her by a department at WSU. They determined she had severe hearing loss. Working through the university, they provided her hearing aids for each ear, again, without cost to her grandparents.

After receiving glasses and hearing aids, the little girl became outgoing and enthusiastic about school. I had moved on to other schools but my nurse friend at the school informed me about her progress.

Making a Difference.

Teachers there realized she was not developmentally challenged. Instead, she was now challenging her teachers. It pleased them that she had advanced to completing second grade by the end of the school year. The intervention of a school nurse and teachers changed her life.

The situation helped me realize the importance and significance a school nurse could make in the life of students. It pleased and excited me to be one of them. I also enjoyed and appreciated the shorter workdays, having holidays off, and the fall and spring breaks from school.

By the end of the school year, I had substituted in many schools. One school I liked was on the west side of Wichita, closer to our home. It was in a low-income area. They needed a full-time nurse, but some nurses preferred a different setting. I felt I could be helpful there, so I applied, and I was accepted.

The Busiest Retired Man.

Before I started in my new position, it was time for me to relax and enjoy summer at home. Ever since I planted radish seeds for Daddy when I was four years old, growing things was one of my pleasures. Now I had time to plant flowers in front of our house and inside the fences around the swimming pool. There was a little room left to plant tomatoes and sweet peppers. I started planting on spring break with early plants and continued throughout the summer.

Bill was the busiest retired man I had ever known. Besides keeping the lawns mowed, he cleaned the pool daily to always be ready for whoever came by. Even though I was home, he continued to do most of the cooking and cleaning, which allowed me to garden or just relax. I so appreciated him.

Interested in the World.

I have been interested in world history ever since our teacher brought the world globe to our one-room school when I was five years old. We learned about the history of our country and Native American history. As a child, we were told we were part Indian. Later, through DNA testing, we learned we were not.

In my life, I read extensively about historic sites, especially about Custer's Little Bighorn Battlefield in Montana. I had wanted to visit the site for years, but there had never been a good time to go. This summer was such a time. When

I mentioned to Bill that I wanted to take the trip, he said, "Let's do it."

After he mowed the lawns and I tended my garden, we packed our suitcases and headed out on the thousand-mile trip to Montana.

Bill and I spent a couple of days touring the battlefield and visiting the museums. We learned that the two-day battle in 1876 was tragic and a terrible mistake by Custer. George Armstrong Custer's army prompted the battle with the Indian tribes peacefully camped there. He lost and died there, along with his entire army. They also killed many Indians. A very sad time in history.

We spent two days on the road each way and took our time going home. Bill especially enjoyed the long, spectacular drive. It made him happy to be driving and "on the road again." The beautiful views of the mountains, valleys, plains, rivers, and lakes were worth the trip. It lives in my memory as one of our best trips, even if I dozed off.

By the time we got home, the lawns needed mowing, and my garden needed tending. And there was lots of laundry to do. Life goes on. But I still had time to relax and enjoy having guests before I went back to work.

Ms. Bonnie and a Clothes Closet.

I was eager to start my nursing position in my own school. The prior year had prepared me well for it. They introduced me to the teachers and students as their new school nurse in our first assembly meeting, where I told the students to call me "Ms. Bonnie."

It was soon apparent that many students were wearing worn clothes and shoes and flip-flops. Because of this, the principal encouraged our social worker and me to set up a clothing room, which we were happy to do. I contacted some of my church friends. They began bringing nice used clothing and shoes in sizes that fit our students.

Concerned about our students not having winter clothes, I also asked my friends to bring warm coats. We soon had a well-stocked closet with clothes to meet the needs of our elementary students.

"Just my belly."

A couple of days after school started a little boy came to my office with a note from his teacher. It said he was not feeling well and was not doing his schoolwork. I had him lie down on the couch, and I took his temperature. It was normal. I asked him if he was hurting anywhere.

He quietly said, "Just my belly. I'm hungry. I didn't have any breakfast." He told me he had had nothing to eat since his school lunch the day before.

I immediately went to the school kitchen and got him a cereal box, a carton of milk, and orange juice. After eating, I sent him back to his classroom with a note to his teacher explaining why he wasn't feeling well.

A couple of mornings later, another little boy came to my office. He also had not eaten since lunch at school the day before. Again, I went to the kitchen to get food for him.

This time the woman working there said, "I can't keep giving you free food like this."

"How much do you want? I'll pay you," I said, annoyed. She gave me the food I asked for.

Our principal was a young woman, very much involved in the student's lives. I told her what the kitchen aide said. The principal said, "I'll take care of her."

Later, when I asked the kitchen for food, they willingly gave me what I asked for. We soon understood the need to solve the hunger problem among our students. No doubt, other students were hungry but just waited until lunchtime to eat.

Our principal, social worker, teachers, and I began working with students and their families. We had school breakfasts, but some families had transportation problems getting their children to school in time for breakfast. Some families did not know there were resources to get food without cost to them when they qualified.

After a few weeks, with families and staff working together, we felt we had our students' hunger problems under control. They could now focus on their studies and learning and making school a fun place to be with their friends.

The Nosebleed.

One of my most memorable and cutest experiences happened after I start at my full-time school. Early winter weather had set in. A little kindergarten boy came to my office. Slowly, he handed me a note from his teacher that said he had a nosebleed.

I set him on the cot and cleaned the blood from his nose and upper lip. Sitting him upright, I put a soft nose clamp on his nose for a few minutes. After removing the clamp and observing the bleeding had stopped, I sent him back to his classroom.

A couple of hours later, he came back to my office with a nosebleed and another note from his teacher. Together, we repeated the previous procedure, and I sent him back to his classroom. But...

About an hour after lunch, the little guy came back to my office with another note. I set him on the cot and began wiping and cleaning his nose again. Then I noticed scratches on his upper lip and around his nostrils.

I asked him, "Are you picking your nose?"

He looked down and answered, "Yeah."

"That's the reason your nose is bleeding. You're scratching your lip and nose. Stop picking your nose."

He looked up at me and quietly but firmly asked, "Then, how'm I gonna get the boogers out?"

I muffled a snicker, and I told him to ask his teacher for some tissue to blow and wipe his nose. I sent him back to his classroom with another note to his teacher. The instructions seemed to work. He never returned to my office.

Improvements Made.

The basic need for shelter was sometimes an issue for our low-income families. Our social worker and I assisted them in locating resources to stabilize their homes. Responding to two of the basic needs: food and clothing, we felt progress was being made.

Working with input from teachers, our school secretaries,

and my work as a nurse, we improved our students' well-being. I was proud to be part of all this.

Catching Up with Family – "Git a job!"

We had not visited Bill's two sisters and two brothers who lived in or near Jefferson City together for many years. Bill had made the trip alone. It was good to see them all again. We had a nice visit with them, and his nieces and nephew for several days.

Bill's youngest brother, Vernon, in his fifties, had Down's Syndrome. He was seven when I first met him. He had a severe speech impediment, but that didn't stop him from talking. I soon understood him better than his siblings.

With Bill's parents' passing, Vern now lived in a cottage with other Down's Syndrome men, supervised by a live-in couple. He was in a make-work job with other developmentally challenged men. Their job was to break down used cardboard boxes for disposal.

We visited him at his workplace, and he was proud to show us around the warehouse. In his broken speech, Vern asked Bill, "What do you do?"

Bill told him, "I'm retired. I don't have a job."

Vern grumbled and said, "Ahh! Git a job!" We spent the evening with him and his friends.

Visiting Uncle Carl.

After a pleasant evening in a motel, Bill and I headed out to his Uncle Carl's farm, an hour's drive away. Bill had many pleasant memories of growing up close to his grandparents' farm. He especially liked attending the neighborhood square dances and hearing the local musicians and German music on records on the wind-up record player.

Uncle Carl didn't a have phone yet. When we drove up to the house at mid-day, he seemed pleased to have company, and that we brought lunch with us. Visitors didn't usually bring food. We spent the afternoon visiting, and when it came time to feed and milk the cows, Bill was glad to help.

While they did that, I fired up Carl's wood-burning cookstove and had supper ready when they returned. I fried potatoes and fresh, sweetened green apples in cast-iron skillets. I found some ham in his fridge and made biscuits from scratch, too.

We visited long into the evening before going to bed in the hot upstairs bedroom. With the long, memorable day behind us, we went to sleep, waking up early to the rooster's crowing. The delights of farm living.

Bill helped his uncle with the morning chores, and I fired up the stove again to cook a big breakfast of bacon and fresh eggs. Biscuits with honey and coffee brewed on the stove topped off our meal.

After relaxing and visiting a couple of days, Bill knew his uncle needed to get back to work in his fields and garden. We needed to head home, too. It was time to travel back through the beautiful hills of Missouri.

Head Lice Epidemic.

The summer passed quickly, and it was time to begin

another year of school nursing.

When school started, there was not much change in the teaching staff from last year. We knew most of the kids, except the new kindergartners. Hunger and clothing concerns were addressed, and the students were enjoying our pleasant learning environment.

As the year progressed, head lice became apparent. With heavy coats and closer contact with each other, head lice became an epidemic in the Wichita school system. If I found them on our students, I had to send them home until they were treated, and I cleared them to return to their class.

The treatments, both prescription and over the counter, were expensive. Some families could not afford them. If the head lice invasion became epidemic in a school, the principal had to close it. Sadly, our school had to close one time. Some other schools were closed more than once.

Closing a school was traumatic for both students and parents. First, the students didn't have school meals. Some working parents didn't have childcare. Even a few days of closure interfered with classroom learning. Teachers and students struggled to stay on track with learning plans.

After closure ended, their teacher checked each returning student before going back to class. They sent questionable cases to me for final evaluation and approval to return to class. Hoping we would never suffer another closing, I was determined to practice preventive care to divert another one.

Researching Preventive Care.

Throughout my nursing career, I had focused on

preventive care. So, I began researching to learn more about head lice. I wanted to prevent infestations in individual students, to decrease absenteeism.

I learned a significant fact in treating head lice and their live eggs (nits) in my scientific research. High heat kills both head lice and their nits.

Head lice laid several eggs each day and attached them to the scalp at the base of a hair follicle. The eggs are pale, the size of a pinhead, and can hardly be seen. The egg hatches in about seven days, leaving an empty shell, which is more visible than the unhatched egg.

If the hair shaft to which the shell is attached has grown even a fraction of an inch, they often considered it viable, but it is not now live. In my practice, I used this reliable information to determine whether the nits or eggs found were live and viable.

Since heat killed head lice and nits, I kept a hairdryer in my office. When I concerned about a student possibly having live lice, I used the hairdryer on their hair and scalp. I wanted to assure no viable lice could remain alive there.

As cold weather began, the students hung their heavy coats on hooks where they touched each other. I encouraged the teachers to have the students hang their coats on the back of their chairs to prevent their coats from touching; one more preventive intervention.

I encouraged parents to run their children's coats in their clothes dryer when they came home from school. Some families did not have clothes dryers.

I also informed the parents of the preventive benefits of using a hairdryer on the child's hair and scalp. The procedure reduced the chances of becoming infected with head lice and having to miss school for treatment.

Their teacher often sent a student to my office when they noticed a nit clinging to a hair shaft. When I checked it, and the nit was not close to the scalp, I knew it was an empty eggshell. Using these preventive interventions, our school reduced our head lice infections to a minimum.

Time for Christmas Break.

Although it was stressful at school, I looked forward to time spent with our families during the holidays. We celebrated Thanksgiving early as before. We had our large roasted turkey and my rice dressing and all the other goodies our families loved to make. And on Friday after Thanksgiving, Bill and I set up our six-foot permanent Christmas tree. We enjoyed decorating it together for our first time.

With life so busy, I continued doing most of my Christmas shopping by mail-order catalog. Bill helped me wrap the presents as they arrived. Because of the wonderful addition of grandkids, we soon had piles of presents under our tree.

In our tradition, we celebrated with our families the Sunday before Christmas. After opening the many gifts, we feasted on our buffet dinner, visited, and caught up with each other, then indulged again on our favorite desserts. No one ever starved. Another of my treasured parts of these get-togethers was when some of us sang the beautiful old carols a Capella, in four-part harmony.

By late afternoon, we started giving goodbye hugs, and our families left to celebrate later Christmas Day.

Bill and I considered visiting my three brothers and their families in Republic, Missouri between Christmas and New Year's Day.

At school, the students were singing Christmas songs in their music classes and in the halls. The students presented a beautiful Christmas program of music and poetry one evening for their families and friends. The auditorium was packed, and Santa paid a visit.

On Wednesday, we were all so excited to go home to celebrate Christmas Eve on Thursday and Christmas Day on Friday. We would not return until next year, January 4.

A Malpractice Threat.

I hurried home from school. The aroma of the wood-burning fireplace and Bill's cooking greeted me. So did Bill. Then he gave me a handful of Christmas cards and letters that had arrived that day.

Looking through them, I noticed an official letter from the Kansas State Board of Nursing. The Board monitored nursing practice in the State of Kansas. They also issued our nursing license every two years after completing the required continuing education classes for licensure. Receiving a letter from them was unusual. Nervously, I opened it.

A paraphrased summary of the letter stated: You have been reported to the Kansas State Board of Nursing for a case of malpractice that requires further investigation.

I collapsed in my recliner. Bill saw I was sobbing, shocked, and devastated. I explained that reporting a nurse to the Board for malpractice usually meant they had caused severe harm or death to someone in their nursing practice.

Somehow, I gained control of my emotions and called the Board office. I got a recording stating the office would be closed until January 4. Until then, I would not know what the complaint of malpractice against me was about.

Bill tried to assure me that everything would turn out alright. But I had known of charges brought against other nurses. When proven, they could lose their nursing license. Or, even worse, be charged with a crime. I was too devastated to take the trip to see our family in Republic that we had been planning.

We didn't tell anyone else, not even our kids, their families, church friends, or our pastor. I asked the pastor to find someone to teach my Sunday morning Bible class. I just couldn't deal with anything else. There was no easy way to get through the week ahead until I could call and talk with the Board officials. Bill tried to make things easier by taking us out to eat at nice restaurants. Through it all, he was suffering along with me.

I Had Not Done Wrong.

On Monday morning, January 4, I called the Kansas State Board of Nursing and reached an official. They would send me a follow-up letter in the mail. I became emotional and begged them to give me some idea of the charges.

The official put me on hold, and I held my breath, shaking inside. After a long pause, he said, "A teacher had filed a complaint against you, that you were sending students back to the classroom with nits in their hair."

That was it? Sobbing, I thanked the official for his help and hung up.

Bill was standing close by and could see I was smiling through my tears. I dressed for work, but he worried about me driving when I was so emotional. I controlled myself, gave him a reassuring smile, and went to the school. I felt confident in how things would work out; I knew I had not done wrong.

When I told my principal about the letter I received and about the complaint, she told me she had not known about the charges against me. She seemed indignant and said to keep it quiet, that she would take care of the situation. Trusting her, I went to my office and began my day as a school nurse like normal.

I told my nurse friend from WSU who had convinced me to go into school nursing. It angered her that the Board accepted the erroneous complaint for review and had sent me the letter. She assured me that my reputation as a school nurse would not be affected, and my nurse practitioner license was not at risk.

Commendations in Support.

A few days later, our principal said she received letters of commendation from my fellow school nurses and former instructors and professors from WSU. Some of them had mailed over twenty duplicate copies of the letters to my home. I truly appreciated their support.

I heard that the Kansas State Board of Nursing also received letters of commendation on my behalf. The letters complained about the inaccurate charges brought against me. Within a few weeks, the Board notified me they had nullified the charges.

It remained a mystery to me. Why would the Board consider the letter the teacher sent to them, claiming my malpractice? The incident was the most traumatic in my nursing career and possibly in my life. For me, to consider that I may have caused a patient harm, or worse, was devastating.

A Final Decision.

But positive things were now happening. My nursing license was up for renewal in March, my birth month. I had already completed the continuing education classes to apply for the Nurse Practitioner License renewal for two more years.

All the stress and trauma caused me to think about what was most important to me. I enjoyed the nursing career I had worked so hard for, but Bill and our family were my priority. Our grandkids were now spending more time with us. And Bill and I treasured our road trips, especially to the historic sites we both enjoyed.

I was sixty-eight years old, enjoying excellent health, and Bill's health was good. We spent time talking about our future together. He expected me to do what I wanted, which I decided was spending more time with him and our family. And traveling and sightseeing.

Choosing to resign from my school nurse position was easy. I learned I had a small State retirement through the school district. I also started drawing my Social Security.

With our combined income, we were financially stable. It was the greatest freedom I had ever known in my life.

I told my principal about my decision. She congratulated me on a well-earned retirement and wished me well. Our school staff, led by our secretaries, held a big retirement party for me at the end of the school year. They invited my fellow school nurses and former co-workers. I told them I was not retiring from nursing and planned to keep my license current, intending to work part time when I chose to work. The party lasted throughout the afternoon and was another special memory in my life.

Bill was so excited and pleased, feeling our freedom, too. We could go on longer trips when the weather was nice in the spring and summer and enjoy the colorful scenery wherever we went. For my five years of school nursing, we could not travel in the spring or fall.

Chapter Eleven
GOLDEN ANNIVERSARY

"I didn't know..."

Our 50th wedding anniversary was coming up in May 1999. It was also the year for the family reunion my family had held every two years since Mom's passing in 1969. We always held the reunion near the Fourth of July. Looking forward to both, I sent out over one hundred invitations to extended family and friends. I let everyone know we would celebrate our special anniversary then and renew our wedding vows.

I had heard other couples brag about receiving large monetary gifts for the 50th wedding anniversaries. We didn't want to do that. I had it printed on the invitations: Please respect our request for no gifts. Almost everyone did.

Amazed, I could not have imagined the response we received.

Then, one day I overheard Bill saying to someone, "I didn't know I had to renew my marriage license every fifty years." His sense of humor never failed.

Renting a Place.

I had always rented a Wichita park facility for our two-day weekend reunions. This time, we needed a place to get together on Saturday for our reunion and buffet supper. On

Sunday we would have a morning church service, a buffet dinner provided for us, and renew our vows at two o'clock in the afternoon.

To ensure having what we needed, I started checking around in early April. I learned about the Caprice Ballroom in Goddard, close to our home. The ballroom was only available for private banquets and dances by large organizations. I reasoned, "My family is about the largest organization that I know of." And we planned to have their requirements: a banquet and a dance. Plus, we were adding the church service and the anniversary celebration.

I met with the manager to discuss renting the ballroom. He told me that the best-paying service they offered was their open bar, where alcoholic beverages were served. When I explained we did not want the open bar, he said the ballroom could not be available to us. I countered with an offer to increase the rental charge and keep the bar closed. He agreed to rent it with one stipulation: We would hang curtains in front of the closed bar.

The ballroom would serve a Saturday evening buffet and a Sunday dinner buffet after the church service. When our celebration concluded, there would be additional charges to cover the buffets. Not a problem.

Pre-celebration party.

On Saturday morning before May 14, our kids and grandkids gathered at our home. We arranged for a photographer to take family group pictures in the beautiful outside setting near our house by the lake. The photos have meant a lot to us over the years.

1999 Bonnie and Bill with their kids

1999 Bonnie and Bill with their grandkids

After the photo session, we returned to our house and had our usual potluck of family foods we enjoyed. Then I served the chocolate sheet "Wedding Cake" I made in honor of the day. Following that, everyone swam in the pool Bill kept clean and ready. It was a fun-filled, relaxing time with everyone.

House Full of Guests.

There would be guests staying with us at our house for the weekend or longer of our reunion/celebration. We were excited to invite my brother Al and his wife to stay with us. They lived in California, and I had only seen him a few times since he left home in 1940. Their two grown daughters stayed in motels but visited our home.

I also invited my brother Jess and his wife from Missouri to stay with us. Jess was in a wheelchair. My brother James and his wife stayed in our camper, so he could help Jess get up and down the stairs in his wheelchair in our split-level house.

Some family members couldn't afford motels and we invited them to stay with us as well. We had two more bedrooms and two sofa beds. Others brought sleeping bags and slept on the floor. We ended up with over twenty house guests and enjoyed the slightly chaotic experience.

Family members from several states, including east and west coast, stayed with relatives in Wichita and local motels.

1999 House full of guests

Bunny Hop and Hokey Pokey.

By Saturday afternoon, the huge ballroom became packed with our guests. There was no shortage of entertainment. My brothers brought their guitars, and someone was singing and playing throughout the afternoon into the evening. Many joined in, including me.

1999 Singing together

There were Bunny Hop lines throughout the day, and one or more groups did the Hokey Pokey with lots of eager participants. But some guests just enjoyed visiting with family members. Mom had forty-two grandchildren, so many cousins were visiting who had not seen each other for a long time.

Bunny Hop line

In the late afternoon, the ballroom people set up the buffet. We were all hungry and ate while enjoying my brother's live entertainment. After a long, tiring, but pleasant day we headed home or to our various sleeping arrangements to get a good night's sleep. It would be a big day tomorrow.

Standing Room Only.

Bill and I, and everyone staying with us, woke early to prepare and enjoy a large buffet breakfast. Then we headed to the ballroom for the church service.

Childhood friends of mine came from out of state and stayed in motels. They would attend the church service, presented by my youngest brother, Walt. All the guests were invited to our Sunday buffet dinner before the renewal of our vows.

When the time came for the church service, the seats were packed, and guests were standing in the back of the room to watch the service. Friends from Wichita and Lake Waltanna were there, too. Walt's wife played the piano while we sang the preferred old hymns.

Following the service, the ballroom staff served our buffet dinner. Our pastor and friends from our church were also invited to join us for the meal and stay for our ceremony.

Pronounced Husband and Wife ... Again.

The time had finally arrived, and the "wedding party," Bill, our four kids, and I dressed for the ceremony. I had made a burgundy silk dress for me and aqua bridesmaid's dresses for Kathi and Susan. Our two great-granddaughters wore pretty dresses as flower girls. John and Charlie wore short-sleeved white shirts and ties, while Bill wore a nice sports jacket, I made for him.

Dressed now, we headed to where the ceremony would take place. Walt was waiting for us, and a great-nephew with a beautiful voice sang for us.

Just as we had fifty years ago, Bill and I said our wedding vows and meant them. We gave each other rings again, and we kissed as Walt pronounced us husband and wife. After all the work and fuss, it was such a short ceremony. But it was worth it and the memories we would treasure in the years ahead.

Bill was smiling, and I thought about his teasing comment a couple of months before. I knew he was feeling pleased to have "renewed his marriage license for another fifty years." This was a man I would love forever.

Wedding party: Bonnie and Bill, their kids, and grandkids

Bonnie with her brothers

Bonnie and Bill renewing their vows

A New Beginning for Us.

Ceremony finished, the wedding party walked to back of the ballroom, where we had beautifully decorated sheet cakes to serve our guests. After Bill and I gave each other a bite of cake, we served our guests for over an hour.

The guests again formed groups to do the Hokey Pokey and lined up to do the Bunny Hop. Once more, my brothers played their guitars and sang with others playing along on the piano. It was such a fun time, with much laughter.

Bill and Bonnie having some fun

When the ballroom closed late that afternoon, there were many happy and tearful goodbyes. We didn't always know when or if we would see each other again. But we vowed to keep in touch. Bill and I headed home to a houseful of company. My brothers and their wives would stay with us for many days before returning to their homes.

I was curious about how many attended the family

reunion and our 50th wedding anniversary celebration. After collaboration with others, we determined over four hundred guests attend our two-day event.

The celebration was over, but Bill and I would continue to celebrate our marriage. We could enjoy our retirement, treasuring the time we had together. We both felt like this was a new beginning for us. It was.

Although Bill has passed on up to Heaven now, I still celebrate our life together. I know I will see him again someday.

Childhood Dreams - Completed

_X_   Marry a good-looking man and have good-looking children. (I did, and they were!)

_X_   Have two boys and two girls. (I did.)

_X_   Be a nurse. (I did.)

_X_   Fly an airplane. (I did.)

Chapter Twelve

LIVING

Trees and grass and fields of wildflowers.
Playing and sleeping.
Mom cooking:
Eggs, milk, biscuits, molasses, gravy, cracklins, greens,
mushrooms.
Brothers everywhere; pampering, disciplining and teasing.
Daddy was sick; he couldn't hold me.
The doctor came; Daddy had blood poisoning, fever.
The days were hot, and the nights.
The neighbors stood over Daddy fanning, day and night.
July, '34; Missouri, misery.

The doctor came.
My brothers said Mom was tired; she couldn't hold me.
The doctor picked me up and told me I had two new baby
brothers.
I already had brothers of every size.
A baby brother, brothers about my size and big brothers
like Daddy.
Hot; no rain, only hot days and nights and fussy, crying
babies.
The neighbors stood over them and Mom, fanning day and
night.

The doctor came; he left quietly.
The neighbors were there, quiet and unsmiling.
Grandpa said the baby had gone to Heaven to be with
God.
But Daddy built a box and they put him in the ground.
The man in strange clothes said the baby's spirit was in
Heaven.
I hoped my spirit didn't go to Heaven.
I was barely three.

The rains came!
We had to shoo the chickens inside so they wouldn't drown.
They didn't know what rain was.
Now the chickens would lay eggs again, the cows would
give milk again.
We romped and splashed and played in the rain.
Too late, the rain, for Spring and Summer crops; they never
came up.
Daddy and my brothers planted acres of turnips; they grew
fast.
We ate turnips and all the animals ate turnips.
The cow's milk tasted like turnips, the sausage tasted like
turnips.

Winter winds same through the wooden floors and around
the doors and windows.
Mom and Daddy slept with my little brother and the baby
and me.
To keep us warm, because the wood fires went out at night.
Also, to keep us protected from the rats.

Spring! Everything in the house was loaded on the wagon;
we had no car.
Daddy and my big brothers were building a new home.
Made from trees they cut and sawed at the saw mill.
Just framework and boxing; he'd build a better one later.
They had to hurry and plant spring crops.
Days of hard work and play; our own swimming hole.
Nights of fun, laughter and singing, from somewhere a
guitar.
Acres of trees: walnut, persimmon, sycamore, hickory and
pawpaw.
Blackberries by the tub full, watermelon, tomatoes,
potatoes and corn.
The first fruits and vegetables I could remember.
Now we had enough to eat.

Mom was tired; my brothers helped her in the kitchen.
The doctor came, carrying his black bag.
My brothers told me doctors don't bring babies, and why.
The new baby was a boy; now there were ten brothers.
One girl; I was four years old.

Winter winds whistled through the wooden floors and
through the boxing.
At night we snuggled together in beds to keep warm.
Somewhat contented, lots of love, nobody sick.

Spring!
My brothers went swimming on Easter Sunday, always.
Even if they had to break the skifts of ice on the
swimming hole.

Daddy went to town to get seeds; horseback, we had no
car.
Someday I would get to go to town where big people go.
We made a garden, barefoot; everyone worked and played.

School!
Finally! I get to go to school where my brothers go.
The first special thing that ever happened to me.
New crayons for me, my own tablet and pencil!
Mom made me a new chambray dress.
My big brother carried me the two miles on his back.
Those girls in frilly dresses, blonde curls, blue eyes and pink
skin.
I didn't look like other girls look!
With straight bobbed, brown hair, dark eyes, dark, tanned
skin; and barefoot.
Girls play different games than boys: jacks, hopscotch,
jump rope.
So many things to see: a bicycle, a piano, jello, the teacher's
car.
Books about strange people that were a different color than
I was.
Books about lands far away.

They started Church in the schoolhouse on Sunday.
I had never heard of church; the family went in the wagon.
The preacher said we should love thy neighbor as thyself.
Strange; I had never heard of that.
He gave me a little Bible.
I learned to read; the first chapter of Genesis.
Now I knew most everything; I was almost nine.

Spring came.
Mom was tired, in bed; my brother helped with the cooking
and homework.
My big brother woke me one morning.
He said we had a new baby sister; he couldn't fool me!
I ran to Mom, who was still in bed.
She showed me; the baby was a girl!
My world was complete; what more could I want.

War! What was that?
Handsome brothers in uniform, going off to protect us,
Mom said.
Five of them! But they could die!
Hadn't Grandma died?
She was grouchy, didn't like little kids, and smoked a smelly
pipe.
I tried to cry when she died, because Daddy was crying, but
I couldn't.
How I prayed for my brothers, though I wasn't sure how to
pray.
Night after night, year after year, always remembering.
They all came back! Had God really heard?
Daddy worked building defense plants during the war; we
moved many times.
Now that the war was over, we could stay in one place.
I could go to one school; I was fourteen.

I was no longer mistaken for one of the boys; that was
nice.
It had been fun to be a tomboy or a girl, as I chose.
It was good to be almost a woman.

I had become somebody special in school; good grades,
good in sports.
I was outstanding for the first time; it felt good.

Jesus became real to me!
A peace and joy I had never known before!

Daddy. They said he died instantly in the car wreck.
He was so special to me.
He taught me to hope and dream.
I was sixteen.

I didn't want a boyfriend; I had heard my brothers talk
about girls!
Bill! He would be a friend; the best friend I could ever have.
I was sixteen! What was happening?
It was good to be a woman.
I was eighteen; we were married.
Bill, my best friend, my lover, the father of my children.
Two sons and two daughters, in that order, in four years.
Time moves so fast!

War again! What kind of war is this?
A son AWOL? It may be said, "The enemy is us."
How brave he was to stand by his convictions!
Another son saved by the lottery.
Both now safe! But what of all the other wasted lives?
"The enemy is us!"

Can it be; our little girls have grown up?
Just yesterday I was braiding their pigtails.

Mom, the tiny matriarch! She has gone to be with her Jesus!
She taught me to have compassion for others.
So much of her is still with me; I shall always miss her.

What? I'm a grandmother?
But grandmothers are old and grouchy and strange; not this
one!
I am a woman, a daughter, a mother, a sister, a scholar!
I am a wife, a friend and a lover.
For Bill and me, life is good; most of it is still ahead of us!

Bonnie Lacey Krenning
June 1975

Read more from
Bonnie Lacey Krenning

An Old Country Girl's Beginning
My First 90 Years: Book 1

An Old County Girl Makes a Family
My First 90 Years: Book 2

Made in the USA
Monee, IL
24 February 2023

27912425R00108